CONCILIUM

THEOLOGY IN THE AGE OF RENEWAL

CONCILIUM

CONCILIUM/VOL. 7

CHURCH HISTORY

HISTORICAL PROBLEMS OF CHURCH RENEWAL

Volume 7

CONCILIUM
theology in the age of renewal

PAULIST PRESS/GLEN ROCK, NEW JERSEY

NIHIL OBSTAT: Joseph F. Donahue, S.J., S.T.L.
Censor Deputatus

IMPRIMATUR: ⊠ Bernard J. Flanagan, D.D.
Bishop of Worcester

Aug. 19, 1965

The Nihil Obstat and Imprimatur are official declarations that a book or pamphlet is free of doctrinal or moral error. No implication is contained therein that those who have granted the Nihil Obstat and Imprimatur agree with the contents, opinions or statements expressed.

Library of Congress Catalogue Card Number: 65-26792

Suggested Decimal Classification: 270

BOOK DESIGN: Claude Ponsot

Paulist Press assumes responsibility for the accuracy of the English translations in this Volume.

PAULIST PRESS
EXECUTIVE OFFICES: 304 W. 58th Street, New York, N.Y. and
     21 Harristown Road, Glen Rock, N.J.
Executive Publisher: John A. Carr, C.S.P.
Executive Manager: Alvin A. Illig, C.S.P.
Asst. Executive Manager: Thomas E. Comber, C.S.P.

EDITORIAL OFFICES: 304 W. 58th Street, New York, N.Y.
Editor: Kevin A. Lynch, C.S.P.
Managing Editor: Urban P. Intondi

Printed and bound in the United States of America by The Colonial Press Inc., Clinton, Mass.

CONTENTS

PART IV

CHRONICLE OF THE LIVING CHURCH

PREFACE

Roger Aubert/*Louvain, Belgium*

Anton G. Weiler/*Utrecht, Netherlands*

I n a world striding toward the future, many consider history a somewhat outmoded pastime. Church history shares in this lack of appreciation, the more so as priests, committed to action, come to look upon it as a luxury for the sole indulgence of intellectuals. Yet now, more than ever, Church history has its place in a theological publication that has adopted the attitude outlined by Vatican Council II: an adjustment to the contemporary demands of the ministry, to be achieved in an ecumenical spirit by a return to the sources. In the course of her existence the Church has always striven to adapt herself to the civilizations in which she found herself successively embodied. Thus, from time to time, she moves toward an *aggiornamento* that is manifested in her life and in her teaching of divine revelation; new situations urge such an updating at the peril of a creeping sclerosis.

It is therefore vital for her to realize why and how, in certain definite instances, some of her attempts succeeded while others failed, or ended (as the Reformation of the 16th century) in catastrophe. It is equally important that the patristic, conciliar or liturgical sources which must guide contemporary research be placed in their true context so that their exact meaning and true bearing can be established. This alone can give a return to the sources its authentic character.

1

Finally, we cannot overlook the fact that the Church, whose structure is the focus of present-day theological discussion and ecumenical dialogue, is an historical reality, is involved in history. As Father Congar said recently, "Many inadequacies of our concrete ecclesiology can be discovered and overcome, and many obstacles cleared only by an historical study of situations, teachings and customs which have become attitudes affecting our daily lives."

The volume annually devoted to Church history in *Concilium* seeks to provide theologians, who must inspire those who work in the pastoral and ecumenical fields, with some particularly topical aids in the important work of unfolding current thought and presenting it to the age-old life of the Church.

PART I

ARTICLES

Brian Tierney/*Ithaca, N.Y.*

Collegiality in the Middle Ages

In their writings on ecclesiology medieval theologians and canonists constantly strove to hold together in harmonious balance a variety of ancient doctrines concerning the nature of the Church which, taken in isolation from one another, might seem unrelated or even mutually contradictory. Above all, they emphasized the primacy of the pope, the collegial authority of the clergy and the corporate structure of the whole Christian community. Already in Hugh of St. Victor's *De Sacramentis*, "the first complete theological treatise of the medieval schools" (ca.1134), all three elements received due recognition. "All things that are spiritual and attributed to the spiritual life," wrote Hugh, "belong to the power of the supreme pontiff." "Among the clergy, however, to whose office belong those things that are the goods of the spiritual life, is divine power." "What then is the Church but the multitude of the faithful, the assembly of Christians?" [1]

[1] Migne, *Patrologia Latina*, cols. 176, 417-8. "All things that are terrestrial and attributed to terrestrial life belong to the power of the king. All things that are spiritual and attributed to the spiritual life belong to the power of the supreme pontiff." "Among laymen, to whose attention and foresight belong matters that are necessary to life on this earth, power is of an earthly nature. Among the clergy, however, to whose office belong those things that are the goods of the spiritual life, is divine power." "What then is the Church but the multitude of the faithful, the assembly of Christians?"

5

Hugh's contemporary, St. Bernard of Clairvaux, likewise insisted equally in his *De Consideratione* on the dignity of the papal office, on the duty of the pope to uphold the divinely bestowed authority of other bishops, and on his overriding obligation to serve humbly, as a faithful pastor, the whole flock of Christian people entrusted to his care. It was, however, yet a third writer of the 1130's, the canonist Gratian, whose work gave the greatest impetus to the development of ecclesiology during the next century. This will not seem surprising if we remember Maitland's dictum that "in no other age since the classical days of Roman law had so large a part of the sum total of intellectual endeavor been devoted to jurisprudence".

Gratian's *Decretum,* which appeared ca. 1140, was a massive compilation of canonical sources—early patristic texts, canons of councils, decrees of popes—and it became accepted during the middle years of the 12th century as a standard work, universally used in the schools of Christendom for the teaching of canon law. The jurists who commented on Gratian's texts found themselves face-to-face with the whole story of the Church in the world for a thousand years, obliged to interpret it as best they could in the light of their own beliefs and experience. Lacking any refined techniques of historical criticism, they had recourse to dialectical argumentation, seeking to weave together in scholastic syntheses all the different insights into the nature of the Church that Gratian had collected from so many centuries and so many sources.

The 12th-century Decretists, the generation of great jurists who first gave a single law to the universal Church, brought to their task an extraordinary intellectual vitality. Indeed, their attempts to give an appropriate juridical form to the ancient doctrine of the Church as the Body of Christ may well be regarded as the most significant of all the medieval contributions to the concept of collegiality. Too much has been written in modern times about the evils of legalism in the Church. The congregation of the faithful, as a corporate, visible society, needs a body of constitutional law. At the end of the Middle Ages, as in more

recent times, it was not the existence of law as such but the un-
imaginative enforcement of imperfect laws and of bad customs
that distorted the structure of Christ's Church.

The most mature works in the Decretist tradition were written
around 1200 in an age dominated by the greatest of the medieval
lawyer-popes, Innocent III (1198-1216). The canonists of that
time inevitably based their discussions of the structure of the
Church on Christ's words to Peter, "Thou art Peter, and upon
this rock I will build my Church, and the gates of hell shall not
prevail against it. And I will give thee the keys of the kingdom
of heaven . . ." (Matt. 16, 18-19). It was universally agreed
that these words established Peter and his successors as heads of
the Church on earth. But the "keys" which were promised to
Peter were commonly identified with the power to remit sins
that Christ later conferred on all the apostles when he said,
"Whose sins you shall forgive, they are forgiven them . . ."
(John 20, 23). Gratian therefore explained that, "When Christ
would give to all the apostles an equal power of binding and
loosing he promised to Peter the keys of the kingdom of heaven
before all and on behalf of all." And to support this view he
quoted a text of St. Augustine: "When Peter received the keys
he signified the holy Church." [2] The Decretists commonly accepted Gratian's explanation, adding however that the "equal
power" Peter shared with the other apostles was a power of
orders and that in jurisdiction Peter was superior from the beginning. Thus, in a profoundly Catholic spirit, they saw in the
very words that had established papal primacy a source also of
episcopal authority in the Church.

There was another ambiguity in the famous Petrine text that
attracted the attention of the canonists. Christ promised to Peter
or, we may say, to all the apostles the power of the keys. Yet it
was not Peter or the apostolic college but the Church itself which,
according to the word of Christ, was to endure down all the ages,
indefectible, prevailing against the "gates of hell". The particular

[2] *Decretum Gratiani, Corpus Juris Canonici* I (ed. Aemilius Friedberg),
C. 24, q. 1 dictum post c. 4.

problem for the Decretists was that certain texts of Gratian's collection identified the *Romana ecclesia* as the indefectible Church which, since the days of Christ, had preserved immaculately the true Catholic faith, while certain other texts told of particular popes who had sinned and erred in the past. (Gratian, like his contemporary, St. Bernard, was deeply conscious of a possible contrast between the dignity of the papal office and the human failings of the mortal men who occupied it.)

The Decretists explained Gratian's apparently conflicting texts by distinguishing between two meanings of the term *Romana ecclesia* and by further developing St. Augustine's doctrine of the pope as a symbol of the Church. It will suffice to quote by way of example the words of Huguccio, teacher of Innocent III and greatest of all the canonists who were writing at the end of the 12th century: "Christ said to Peter as a symbol of the Church (*in figura ecclesiae*) 'I have prayed for thee Peter that thy faith may not fail'. . . . In the person of Peter the Church was understood, in the faith of Peter the faith of the universal Church which has never failed as a whole nor shall fail down to the day of judgment." And again, "Wherever there are good faithful people, there is the Roman Church. Otherwise you will not find a Roman Church in which there are not many stains and many wrinkles." And once more, "The Roman pope may have sometimes erred, but not the Roman Church which is understood to be not the pope alone, but all the faithful." [3]

The Decretists were not theologians, primarily concerned with the supernatural life of the Church, but jurists whose main task was to explain its institutional structure. Hence, once they had decided that Christ's indefectible Church was the whole congregation of the faithful, the problem arose for them of determining

[3] The various canonical texts mentioned in the article are printed and discussed with additional bibliography in B. Tierney, *Foundations of the Conciliar Theory* (Cambridge, 1955); *idem*, "Pope and Council: Some New Decretist Texts," in *Mediaeval Studies* 19 (1957). For the above texts of Huguccio see *Foundations*, p. 35 n. 1; p. 41; and *Mediaeval Studies, op. cit.*, p. 206.

whether any institution of Church government could provide a more certain expression of this Church's unfailing faith than an individual pope. A starting point for the discussion of this question was provided by a text of Pope Gregory the Great (included in the *Decretum at Dist.* 15 c.2), which declared that the canons of the first four General Councils were to be revered like the four Gospels because they were established by universal consent (*universali sunt consensu constituta*).

Gregory, perhaps, meant only that the consensus of the ages had put these particular canons beyond all possibility of doubt but the canonists gave a more concrete, juridical meaning to his word *consensus* by comparing the general council to other collegiate institutions within the Church. Thus Huguccio wrote on the words *universali consensu:* "Here is an argument for a corporate body, that no one may depart from the canonical and common consent of his chapter or college or city." Huguccio also cited the Roman law text: "What touches all is to be judged by all", in order to prove that, when questions of faith were to be decided, representatives of the laity were to be summoned to general councils—for the maintenance of the true faith was a matter that concerned all Christians.[4]

Since, then, the canons of councils were established by consent of the whole Church, they could be taken as expressing the Church's unfailing faith and as binding on the pope himself. This view did not conflict with the doctrine of papal primacy since the pope was necessarily a member of any council, indeed its very head and center. The laws of general councils reflected a consensus of the whole ecclesiastical college but they were also papal laws expressed in their most authoritative form.

Around 1200, therefore, it became a common doctrine of the canonists that an individual pope was bound by the canons of preceding councils "in matters touching the faith and the general state of the Church". There remained the problem of dealing with a pontiff who in fact offended against such canons. The

[4] *Foundations*, pp. 48 n. 2, 49.

Decretists considered the matter as, so to speak, a possible patho-
logical condition in the body of the Church. No one in the days
of Innocent III seriously expected the pope to fall into heresy.
But since the contingency was not impossible it was necessary
that the constitution of a Church that was to endure down all
the ages should make provision for it.

Huguccio refused to admit that there could be a juridical authority in the Church superior to the pope in any circumstances
whatsoever, and he held that if the pope and the fathers of a
council disagreed over some new formulation of doctrine the
opinion of the pope was to be preferred. But if a pope publicly
professed his adherence to a known heresy, and refused to be
corrected, then he could be removed from his office without the
need for a superior judge ever arising. In becoming a heretic the
pope automatically ceased to be a Catholic and, *a fortiori,* ceased
to be head of the Catholic Church. Huguccio also held that a
pope who scandalized the Church by contumacious persistence in
notorious crime also degraded himself from the papacy just like
a heretic.[5]

Another eminent canonist, Alanus, writing at the beginning
of the 13th century, presented a somewhat different point of view.
He held that a general council, pope and fathers together, was
not only the highest teaching authority but also the highest juridical authority in the Church. A pope who offended against a
conciliar canon enacted *lata sententia* could therefore be deposed
as one already legitimately sentenced by a superior judge. This
still did not provide for the case of a pope accused of propounding a novel heresy, not previously condemned. Alanus therefore
suggested that, when a judgment concerning an article of faith
had to be made (but in no other circumstances), a decision by
the members of a council opposed to the pope was to be regarded
as more authoritative than that of the pope himself. A pope who
resisted the decree of the conciliar fathers could be deposed as a
heretic. Alanus added, however, that this could only be the case
because, in the very exceptional circumstances that he was en-

[5] *Ibid.,* pp. 58-63, 248-50.

visaging, a doubt inevitably arose as to whether the occupant of the papal throne was indeed a true pontiff.[6]

Many other canonists around 1200 were discussing these problems with various nuances of thought and expression. The doctrine of a juridical supremacy inhering in pope-and-council was widely held. On the other hand, no canonist taught without reservations that the members of a council separated from the head could exercise jurisdiction over a certainly legitimate pontiff. Some maintained that the conciliar fathers possessed an intrinsic right to decide whether a purported pope was or was not a true pontiff if his conduct gave rise to doubts concerning his status.

The Decretists' debates on such points may seem remote from real life but in fact the problem of a pope accused of propounding a new heresy became a real one in 1336 in connection with John XXII's views on the beatific vision, and the question whether the intrinsic authority of the Church could be exercised through the fathers of a council separated from the pope became a matter of desperate practical urgency after the outbreak of the Great Schism in 1378.

Something of the Decretists' climate of thought was reflected in certain pronouncements and acts of the contemporary Pope Innocent III. In one of his sermons he declared: "While for other sins God alone is my judge, in the one case of a sin against the faith I may be judged by the Church. For he who does not believe is already judged." [7] In 1206 Innocent informed the Bishop of Pisa that the legal privileges held by the clergy in medieval society were not conceded to them as to individuals or for their own advantage but as to an ecclesiastical college (*collegio ecclesiastico*) and for the public welfare.[8] Finally, in 1213, Innocent convoked the Fourth Lateran Council to deliberate on matters concerning "the common state of all the faithful". To it were summoned not only ecclesiastical prelates but also ambassadors of lay princes and representatives of the chapters of collegiate

---

[6] *Mediaeval Studies*, pp. 208-9, 214.
[7] *P.L.*, 217, col. 656.
[8] *Ibid.*, 215, col. 876.

Churches. These latter were required to attend because, wrote Innocent, matters especially touching such chapters would be considered at the forthcoming meeting.[9]

When the Council duly assembled in 1215 it was the greatest representative assembly that the Western world had ever seen. Dogmatic decrees were promulgated and a sweeping program of reform for the whole Church enacted, including a provision that provincial councils should meet regularly in the future. As the reforms gradually took effect and local councils began to meet in various lands of Christendom, it seemed for a time that the Church would find a juridical structure which was ideally suited to its own intrinsic nature and which would reflect the genius for constitutional organization that was such a striking feature of 13th-century society.

Two factors, however, distorted the growth of ecclesiastical government in the later Middle Ages. The first was a continuing conflict of Church and State. This eventually led secularist philosophers to find anti-papal implications in conciliar doctrines that had been propounded in the first place by thoroughly orthodox Catholics. The other distorting factor was an excessive centralization of authority in the Roman curia. The increasing burden of papal taxation and above all the misuse of the pope's power to appoint clerics to benefices all over Christendom—a power that was employed on a vast scale in the 14th century to serve financial rather than pastoral ends—inevitably evoked protests from diocesan bishops who thought that their own ordinary jurisdiction was being centralized out of existence.

However, in spite of these stresses, it was only very slowly that the sounder traditions of the 12th and 13th centuries were abandoned. Gulielmus Durandus the Younger, writing in 1310, passionately defended the collegiate authority of the bishops against the excesses of papal bureaucracy and he thought it desirable that a general council should meet every ten years to consider matters of legislation and taxation affecting the universal Church. But he also acknowledged that the Roman See was head of all

[9] *Ibid.*, 216, cols. 824-5.

the others and that all were bound to follow it "as head and mother of all the Churches".[10] One finds a similar attitude in John of Paris who wrote a treatise against the papal claim to plenitude of power in temporal affairs during the conflict of Boniface VIII and Philip the Fair (ca.1300). He, too, emphasized the corporate nature of the Church, attributed a great role in Church government to the general council and insisted on the divine origin of episcopal authority; but he also wrote: "In the whole Church and the whole Christian people one is supreme, namely the Roman pope."[11]

A radical break with the medieval tradition of ecclesiology came in the writings of William of Ockham. There have been various attempts in recent years to "rehabilitate" Ockham as a respectable Catholic philosopher but, so far as his ecclesiology is concerned, they have not been very successful. Ockham was no doubt sincere in his Christian beliefs but he seems to have been temperamentally incapable of conceiving of a corporate group, even the Church, as anything other than an aggregate of separate individuals. This was not the teaching of St. Paul. It followed for Ockham that Christ's promise to sustain his Church through the ages meant only that somewhere, in some unspecified individual (probably Ockham), the true faith would always survive. Ockham denied that any institution of ecclesiastical government, even a general council, could adequately represent all the scattered individuals who made up the Church. This atomistic view of ecclesiastical society, pressed to its logical conclusion, left no choice but anarchy or despotism. Ockham seems to have preferred anarchy. As his views became more and more pervasive the popes, understandably perhaps, opted for despotism.

Ockham's theories were widely taught, but by no means universally accepted, at the end of the 14th century. The greatest

[10] *Tractatus de Modo Generalis Concilii Celebrandi* (Paris, 1545), p. 163.

[11] J. Leclercq, *Jean de Paris et l'Ecclésiologie du XIIIe siècle* (Paris, 1942), p. 180. "Just as in any diocese there is one bishop who is the head of the Church among those people, so in the whole Church and among all Christian people one is supreme, namely, the pope of Rome."

theorists of the conciliar movement—Gerson, Zabarella, Nicholaus Cusanus—still sought to combine the principle of ecclesiastical collegiality with the doctrine of papal primacy in the structures of Church government that they discussed. But their efforts were frustrated by the radically anti-papal attitude of the little clique of malcontents who claimed to constitute the General Council of Basle in its later stages.

The failure of the medieval Church to achieve a juridical structure consistent with the insights of its greatest thinkers was the supreme tragedy of the later Middle Ages. The downfall of a Catholic conciliarism, rooted in sound medieval ecclesiology, made inevitable the rise of a Protestant individualism alien to the traditional conception of the Church.

Hilaire Marot, O. S. B./*Chevetogne, Belgium*

The Primacy and the Decentralization of the Early Church

T he Constitution on the Church, after dealing in Chapter III with universal collegiality and the concern that every local bishop must have for the Church as a whole, adds a compact but very important paragraph (n. 23), on what might be called "regional collegiality". It clearly indicates a form of pluralism as a principle.[1] According to the council, the bishops have a regional and local responsibility, which is vital for diversity within the Church and which corresponds to a pluralism of organization, based on geographical and historical factors. The aim of this article is to describe the structural variety of the early

[1] "By divine providence it has come about that various Churches, established in various·places by the apostles and their successors, have in the course of time coalesced into several groups, organically united, which, preserving the unity of faith and the unique divine constitution of the universal Church, enjoy their own discipline, their own liturgical usage, and their own theological and spiritual heritage. Some of these Churches, notably the ancient patriarchal Churches, as parent-stocks of the faith, so to speak, have begotten others as daughter Churches, with which they are connected down to our own time by a close bond of charity in their sacramental life and in their mutual respect for their rights and duties. This variety of local Churches with one common aspiration is splendid evidence of the catholicity of the undivided Church. In like manner the episcopal bodies of today are in a position to render a manifold and fruitful assistance, so that this collegiate feeling may be put into practical application" (n. 23): *De Ecclesia: The Constitution on the Church,* with commentary by Gregory Baum (New York: Paulist Press).

Church, to show that this variety did not conflict with the primacy of Rome and that it disappeared only after ten centuries because of a purely incidental application of this primacy in a way that occasionally obscured its true significance.

REGIONAL PLURALISM IN THE CHURCH
UP TO THE 4TH CENTURY

During the first three centuries the basic structure of the Church's organization gradually took shape. Cooperation among the bishops (their collegiality) developed along two main lines: on the one hand, there were the ecclesiastical provinces and on the other, the larger groups that became the patriarchates. The ecclesiastical provinces, emerging toward the end of the 3rd century, were modeled on the civil provinces of the Roman Empire. Before this there were but loose indications: bishops met locally and spontaneously, without following any definite lines.[2] Nevertheless, collegiality is rooted in the uncertain beginnings of the future provinces, mainly on the occasion of episcopal consecrations.[3] The zones of influence of the great Churches (Alexandria, Antioch and, in the West, Rome) also developed gradually and, it would appear, more quickly than most provinces.[4] Thus, for

[2] Cf. K. Lübeck, *Reichseinteilung und kirchliche Hierarchie des Orients bis zum Ausgang des 4. Jahrhunderts* (Münster, 1901). According to the author, the ecclesiastical provinces, following the lines of imperial administration, existed already in the 2nd century and go back to the apostolic age. This thesis, widely accepted until recently, was rebutted by J. Grotz in *Die Hauptkirchen des Ostens* (Rome, 1964), where the criticisms made by Duchesne, Batiffol and Bardy have been brought together. Batiffol, however, is less radical.

[3] A bishop, indeed, is taken into episcopal collegiality through election by neighboring bishops (or, sooner, by the bishops of the same province). Cf. St. Cyprian, *Ep. 67*, 5: "Therefore the custom, based on divine tradition and apostolic practice, must be diligently observed and maintained, that, with us as in all the provinces, all the bishops of the same province come to the ordination and to the people of the candidate, and that the bishop be elected in the presence of the people who have a sound knowledge of each one's life and can judge each one's actions by his manner of living." This rule, made law at Nicaea, has remained fundamental.

[4] This is the view, particularly, of J. Grotz, *op. cit., passim.*

instance, the councils of Alexandria show the authority of the great See of Egypt, while from the middle of the 3rd century the synods of the vast region from the Black Sea to Egypt display the cohesion and the development area of Antioch.[5] Finally, in 314, the first council of the West took place in which Gaul, Italy, Spain, Africa and Great Britain acted in conjunction with Rome, the Apostolic See of the West.[6] This reflects the conditions prevailing in that sector of the Church.

At the "provincial" and "patriarchal" level we can already see, with regard to Rome, three zones[7] that fully developed their own character only toward the end of the 4th century. During the 3rd century, the first can be seen centered around Rome. The second contains the rest of the West, more or less firmly linked with its center. This covers Africa, built up around Carthage (which kept its special relations with Rome because of the historical connection between Rome and Carthage), and also Spain and Gaul whose organization was still backward and whose contact with Rome was based on missionary activity which had started in Gaul in the 3rd century. Third, there is the East, in its origins owing nothing to Rome, where Alexandria and Antioch tended to exercise a predominance which, however diverse, was similar to that of Rome in the West.

With regard to the primacy of Rome it is important to note that, during the period before the Council of Nicaea, Rome was recognized as the center to which doctrinal matters were referred. Its bishop claimed to be the "successor of Peter" toward the mid-

---

[5] There was a council in 252, against Novatian; others took place in 264 and 268, against Paul of Samosata.

[6] "The West and the Roman Church are so closely united that the council considers itself competent to settle points concerning the Church of Rome. The bishop of Rome is requested to let *all* (*i.e.*, all the bishops of the West) know the decisions of the Council of Arles. The council justifies this request by saying that the bishop of Rome 'holds the major dioceses' (*majores dioceses tenet*), an obscure expression that seems to indicate that it was the task of the bishop of Rome to keep in touch with the whole West and to ensure unity of discipline" (P. Batiffol, *Cathedra Petri* [Paris, 1938], p. 51). A similar situation arose in Sardica, in 343.

[7] Further explanations of these zones were given by Batiffol in 1922; cf. *op. cit.*, part I, chapters II and III, pp. 41-79.

dle of the 3rd century,[8] but the other Churches would not understand these prerogatives in quite the same way. Such expressions as "presidency of love" (Ignatius), the "more powerful principality" founded on Peter and Paul (Irenaeus), and "Principal Church" (Cyprian) did not exactly correspond to the Petrine succession as this was probably already understood even in Rome.[9] The same is clear from certain disagreements that arose, for instance, in Asia in 190 on the Easter question and in Africa and Cappadocia in 256 on the question of baptism by heretics. But, in Rome as elsewhere, this primacy was perfectly compatible with diversity of regional organization within the universal Church, and these differences were finally sanctioned by the whole Church at the First Ecumenical Council.

Both the metropolitan and the supra-metropolitan organizations, which, in embryo, go back to the apostolic age, were authoritatively accepted by Nicaea in 325, a fact resulting logically from a homogeneous development. Within the framework of the ecclesiastical province the origin of collegiality is shown (a) by the fact that all the bishops of the province take part in the consecration of a bishop, at least in principle (Can. 4),[10] and (b) in the exercise of this collegiality by holding two provincial councils per year (Can. 5),[11] where matters are settled by the bishops in common. The only real innovation is that a special responsibility is henceforth attached to the office of "metropolitan" (Can. 4). On the supra-metropolitan level, the council referred to the

---

[8] Cf. the letter of Firmilian of Caesarea to Cyprian (*Ep. 75,* 17): "Because he thus boasts of the locality of his See and says that he holds his succession from Peter, on whom the Church's foundation rests"; *ibid.,* "Stephen who says that he occupies the See of Peter through succession".

[9] For the 2nd century, cf. J. McCue, "Roman Primacy and Development of Dogma," in *Theological Studies* 25 (1964), pp. 161-96.

[10] "Above all, it behooves a bishop to be ordained by all the bishops of that province. If this is difficult, either because of haste or the length of the journey, three in any case must meet for the purpose, and the ordination must take place with the knowledge of the absent bishops who must give their consent in writing."

[11] "It was agreed that councils be held in every province twice a year so that these questions can be discussed in common by all the bishops of the province together." "And these councils must be held, one before Lent . . . and the other in the autumn."

regional jurisdiction of Rome,[12] and confirmed equally the regional primacy of Alexandria, Antioch and some other less important Churches.[13]

These measures of the Council of Nicaea were given greater precision in the course of the 4th and 5th centuries,[14] but this is sufficiently well known to excuse further treatment here.

The Primacy of Rome in the 5th Century

In accordance with the proposals sanctioned by the Council of Nicaea the three zones mentioned above developed their position with regard to Rome during the 4th and 5th centuries, that is, precisely at the time when the Roman primacy reached its final stage there. Before dealing with the various regions of the Church we must look in greater detail at this development of the Roman primacy during the 5th century. Rome was privileged by the double apostolicity and the double martyrdom of St. Peter and St. Paul. Though Paul was not excluded, the very presence of Peter's tomb was an important factor in making the popes of the 5th century more and more conscious of their prerogatives. The claims of Rome were asserted particularly in its relations with the West where it played a special part, but occasionally these claims extended to the East. Historians rightly agree that, toward the middle of the 5th century, Rome's assertions of primacy had reached the level of Vatican I. Some historians even attribute some theses of the later "Roman school" to St. Leo, but wrongly so.[15]

[12] Italy, with, perhaps, a reference to the rest of the West.
[13] Alexandria, centralized like Italy; Antioch much less.
[14] The patriarchates of Constantinople and Jerusalem were organized at Chalcedon in 451.
[15] B. Kidd, T. Jalland, W. Ullmann, F. Heiler, C. Vogel. These authors apply to the metropolitans and bishops a text of St. Leo which only concerns the relations of the pope with his vicar at Thessalonica, *Ep. 14,*1: "We trust your charity to take our place in such a way that you are called to share in our solicitude, not in the fullness of our power." For this text, see J. Rivière, "In partem sollicitudinis; évolution d'une formule pontificale," in *Revue des Sciences religieuses* 5 (1925), pp. 210-31. Or the authors misinterpret other texts such as *Ep. 10,* 1.

The phases of development where the doctrinal aspect is sometimes mixed up with certain accidental circumstances may be outlined as follows:[16] the "Apostolic See" (Damasus) assumed with
Siricius (384-398) the "solicitude of all the Churches" (*sollici-
tudo omnium ecclesiarum*); in relation to the Western bishops,
Innocent I claimed jurisdiction of appeal, and demanded that
what are vaguely described as "important matters" (*causae
maiores*) be referred to Rome after the decision of the synods.[17]
Zosimus (417-418) formulated the principle that there is no appeal from the Apostolic See. Boniface I (418-422) asserted that
Rome's jurisdiction extended to the whole East. He used the
metaphor of the head and the members to describe the relations
between Rome and the other Churches.

Leo, and already Celestine before him, saw the pope not
merely as the successor of Peter, but as continuing and identified
with Peter (*Vicarius Petri*). Gelasius (492-496) drew the consequences of Leo's action: the See of Rome is not bound by councils. He also formulated the teaching that the pope is above the
council and forbade any appeal from a papal decision, but this
was in the course of a rather sterile controversy with the East.
Yet while the aspect of the primacy was continually built up,
some popes of the 5th century also occasionally said important
things about the idea of collegiality.[18] I want to stress, however,
that these doctrinal assertions of the primacy are, in the eyes of
these same bishops, perfectly reconcilable with a concrete situation that allows the Churches a high degree of independence with
regard to the See of Rome. This independence continued to show
itself in the three zones at the very moment when the primacy
of Rome was so heavily emphasized, as we shall see now.

[16] Cf. F. Heiler, *Altkirchliche Autonomie und päpstlicher Zentralismus*
(Munich, 1940), which needs strong qualifications. See particularly the
previous footnote.

[17] P. Batiffol, *op. cit.*, p. 58, observes that this competence in *causae
maiores* is itself "an incidental function of the primacy".

[18] On this point, see the excellent study by J. Lécuyer, *Etude sur la
collégialité épiscopale* (Le Puy, 1964).

Suburbicarian Italy

Toward the end of the 4th century provincial organization was completed in the West and the three zones clearly show the kind of relationship they had with the Bishop of Rome. The first zone constitutes the immediate jurisdiction of Rome and is highly centralized. At first it embraces the whole of Italy but, in the second half of the 4th century, it is limited to the suburbicarian regions (peninsular Italy). In practice there are no provinces and no metropolitans. The whole constitutes a single province of which the Bishop of Rome is the metropolitan: he consecrates all the bishops of this vast province himself and the only synod is the "council of Rome" which gathers around his person and is dominated by him. Occasionally the pope himself will restrict the activity of the local bishops; these take a special oath of obedience.[19]

The Various Structures in the West

The second zone consists of the West beyond the suburbicarian region. The main point is that there are ecclesiastical provinces here where the bishops are headed by metropolitans and meet in provincial synods of which the metropolitan is the president, all according to the canons of Nicaea. Within the framework of each province for which the metropolitan is responsible, the bishops are chosen and consecrated. The bishops are incorporated in the body of the Church through this provincial collegiality. In principle the synods and episcopal elections proceed without intervention on the part of Rome; the metropolitans and the bishops of the province receive their jurisdiction on the spot. Rome determines the principal points of law in the Decretals, often at the request of the interested parties. These Decretals are

[19] Cf. P. Batiffol, op. cit., pp. 41-7. For the two last points see the formulae of the Liber Diurnus (ed. Foerster).

the vehicle of its action in the West and the instrument of a uni-
fied discipline there, as the bishops consider it their duty to apply
this legislation. But for the rest they also legislate independently.[20] Rome intervenes in cases of conflict and, in principle, in
the *causae maiores* (the major causes, where metropolitans are
involved).

While appeals to Rome are rather frequent, spontaneous interventions by Rome are still rare. The pope reminds the bishops
of the provincial organization established at Nicaea and even
refers certain matters back to the provincial synod. Far from
taking advantage of rivalries, the popes constantly insist on the
rights of the local Churches and metropolitans in episcopal elections.[21] They also insist on regular meetings of the provincial
synods. "It is certain that in the middle of the 5th century the
individual character of every province found expression in the
councils that were held more or less frequently",[22] and these
councils tend to become inter-provincial councils.

In Gaul the bishops are able to solve many problems among
themselves. During the 6th century, under the Merovingians, the
two facts I have pointed out for the Gallic-Roman period become still more conspicuous: the provincial councils play an important part and alternate with, or are supplanted by, wider,
inter-provincial councils, particularly in the southeast during the
6th century,[23] but above all by national councils which bring
together all the bishops of one or more political dominions.

The First Council of Orleans in 511 under Clovis is the first

[20] Cf. P. Batiffol, *op. cit.,* pp. 47-59. For this organization in 5th-cen-
tury Gaul, see E. Griffe, *La Gaule chrétienne à l'époque romaine,* II:
L'Eglise des Gaules au Ve siècle; and in connection with this a text of
A. Martimort, "La Gaule chrétienne au Ve siècle," in *Bulletin de littérature Ecclésiastique* 59 (1958), especially p. 42.

[21] Cf. St. Leo, *Ep. 10*: "For we do not object to ordinations in your
provinces."

[22] J. Palanque (A. Latreille, E. Delaruelle and J. Palanque), *Histoire
du Catholicisme en France,* I: *Des Origines à la chrétienté médiévale*
(Paris, 1957), p. 64.

[23] Councils which belong to the tradition of the inter-provincial councils
of the region of Arles.

of a long series. The other fact is that these "national councils" [24] constantly insist on regular (at least annual) provincial councils because they are aware of the need for the regular practice of collegiality on the local level. For instance, the Fourth Council of Orleans (541) declares: "Metropolitans must hold a provincial council every year in order to maintain discipline, unity and love." From time to time there are reminders of the traditional rules for episcopal elections. Already in 517 Pope Hormisdas complained to Avitus of Vienne about the failure to hold councils as the canons of Nicaea had demanded. That the ideal was recalled is important even if the circumstances made it difficult to exercise. For, during the 7th century, political divisions, the king's control of the elections and other factors brought about decadence on a large scale.

At the beginning of the Carolingian age St. Boniface reorganized the Frankish Church and restored the councils. This led to the restoration of the metropolitan system and the revival of provincial synods. Soissons in 744 and Verneuil in 755 ordered that "a synod be held twice a year", in March and October, according to the canons of Nicaea. The most important affairs were dealt with in national synods or even, under Charlemagne, empire synods (Aix, etc.), and these synods always stressed the parallel obligation, going back to Nicaea, to hold provincial synods twice, or at least once, a year.

The second zone is therefore characterized by episcopal activity on provincial, regional and national levels, an activity centered on the metropolitan. The metropolitans derive their jurisdiction from their Sees and transmit it to the bishops of their provinces. Communion with Rome implies the intervention of Rome, particularly in order to maintain unity of discipline in the West. Hence the suburbicarian zone and the rest of the West form a kind of Western patriarchate, presided over by the pope.

Nevertheless, the distinction between these two zones became

---

[24] Agde (506), Can. 71; Orléans II (533), Can. 2; III (538), Can. L; IV (541), Can. 37; Eauze (551), Can. 7.

blurred, and through circumstances which, in themselves, had nothing to do with the doctrinal aspect, the West became more and more assimilated to the suburbicarian zone, particularly during the Gregorian reform of the 11th century.[25] The first step was a change in the very meaning of "metropolitan". Up till then the metropolitan had been the keystone of the regional hierarchy and its local structure. This development began by Rome organizing permanent or temporary vicariates "in order to establish closer links with certain regions of its vast patriarchate" (H. Leclercq). Thus Innocent I instituted in 412 a permanent vicariate in Illyria, with real delegation, in order to control that vast region on the frontiers of the East.[26] Then came the temporary vicariates: that of Arles in southeastern Gaul under the ambitious Patroclus was set up by Pope Zosimus in 417-418; difficulties caused it to be suppressed soon but it was revived spasmodically. Then there was the vicariate of Seville, under Pope Simplicius (468-483), with Zeno as vicar of the Apostolic See, in order to ensure discipline throughout Spain; this, too, did not last long. But it is important to note that these delegated vicars were at once given the pallium, which was the symbol of sharing in papal jurisdiction.[27]

In 512, during a brief revival of the vicariate of Arles, St. Cesarius received the title "apostolic vicar" for Gaul from Pope Symmachus, together with the pallium—the first time this was given to a non-Italian bishop. By means of this same honor the popes also brought within their scope the vast mission territories of England and Germany, evangelized by Augustine, Willibrord and Boniface. "These Christian regions constituted for the popes

[25] Certain aspects of this development have been outlined by F. Heiler, *op. cit.*, pp. 229ff. Here, too, his view needs qualification. My outline has been worked out independently, for the most part.

[26] Cf. St. Leo's formula, quoted above. It concerns the patriarchate of Rome and the suburbicarian zone, and not, as Heiler says, Roman jurisdiction over a part of the East, *op. cit.*, p. 207.

[27] The pallium, symbol of autonomy among those who did not receive it from someone else, was, on the contrary, a symbol of dependence for metropolitans who received it from their patriarch or exarch. Cf. G. Morin, "Le Pallium," in *Le Messager des fidèles* (*Rev. Bén.*) 6 (1889), pp. 258-9.

a kind of direct dependency, which widened their original diocese." [28] Augustine received the pallium from St. Gregory, Willibrord from Sergius I. Boniface obtained it from Gregory II and in 722 took the oath of a suburbicarian bishop. Their successors also received the pallium as a sign by which the pope ratified their election and so found themselves in the same situation as the other metropolitans of what had become part of the suburbicarian diocese (Illyria).

The rest of the West, which was in a very different situation, adjusted itself gradually. Among the reform measures of the Frankish Church, St. Boniface made the Council of Soissons decree in 742 that all metropolitans of Germany and Gaul should go to Rome to apply for the pallium. This remained a dead letter until Charlemagne took it upon himself to make the pallium the distinctive mark of almost all metropolitans in the West. For these "archbishops" the pallium became during the 9th century indispensable for the exercise of their jurisdiction. This novelty was by no means imposed by Rome, but was required by the ruler in order to enhance the prestige of his metropolitans.

In actual fact this involved intervention by Rome. "The heads of the old provinces derived their jurisdiction from the See they occupied, but from the 9th century on an act of the pope was necessary to establish them in possession of their rights" (Amann). At first the metropolitans set off in quest of the pallium only after having been consecrated, but the popes considered that the archbishops could not exercise their jurisdiction until after they had received the pallium. This was the position held by Nicholas I (858-867) and John VIII (872-882): there was no true metropolitan office without the pallium, and at the time of the Gregorian reform in the 11th century the archbishop had to apply for the pallium before his consecration. This implied that confirmation of an archbishop's election was reserved to the pope. This is how the theory arose that episcopal jurisdiction was de-

---

[29] For this and the following paragraph, cf. E. Griffe, "Chrétienté médiévale et chrétienté ancienne," in *Bulletin de littérature Ecclésiastique* 62 (1961), pp. 238-9, partly reproduced here.

rived from the pope, since he confirmed the election of the metropolitan who in turn confirmed that of their suffragans. Thus the
original meaning of St. Leo's formula, "called to share in solicitude but not in the fullness of power" (*Vocatus in partem sollicitudinis, non in plenitudinem potestatis*), which was meant for
his vicar-delegate in Illyria, changed and was applied to all
metropolitans and bishops.[29]

Nevertheless, the councils proceeded as before. But from the
Gregorian reform on we notice that papal legates preside over,
or even summon, inter-provincial councils.[30] On the other hand,
the provincial councils, convoked by the metropolitans, follow
the traditional norms, and the obligation to hold them regularly
was recalled by the Fourth Lateran Council in 1215 (Can. 6).
Not until after the reform of Trent did Sixtus V insist that all decisions be submitted to Rome before promulgation.

PLURALISM IN THE EAST

The third zone covers the Eastern half of the Church. We have
already seen that vast supra-metropolitan jurisdictions had been
established there, legalized by the Council of Nicaea on the
ground of ancient custom, a principle extended to other centers
by later ecumenical councils. These jurisdictions were called
patriarchates and have some similarity with the West, if we consider the West as the "Roman patriarchate". Within the framework of each Eastern patriarchate the degree of centralization
varied, certain features reminding one of the suburbicarian re-

[29] Cf. footnotes 15 and 26.
[30] Cf. E. Delaruelle, *Histoire du Catholicisme en France*, I (Paris,
1957), p. 284: "A last reform achieved the transformation of the bishops
into permanent delegates of the Roman court, so docile that legates were
no longer necessary: this is the 'reservatio' . . . , one of the most important being the choice of bishops. Exceptions to electoral regulations
grow more and more numerous. As an empiricist, concerned with effi-
ciency and justice more than with doctrine and logic, the pope no doubt
did not realize the exorbitant character of some of these reform measures."

gion, others, more of the other provinces in the West.[31] Indeed, the prerogatives of these patriarchates must be understood not in relation to Rome, but in relation to their respective metropolitans and bishops.[32] Communion in the faith being secure, these patriarchates enjoyed a very wide autonomy which Rome accepted normally on the basis of conciliar decisions: they administer themselves. The election of the patriarch is completely free. The patriarch's name is communicated to Rome and to the other patriarchs in view of recognition and common agreement. On such occasions the popes sometimes speak of "confirmation". They can, indeed, refuse if the titular is a heretic or the appointment violates canonical procedure.

If in the West conciliar life usually proceeded without Roman intervention, this holds still more for the East, where it differed somewhat from the West; canonical legislation and the functioning of discipline developed accordingly. In short, interventions by Rome in virtue of the primacy remained exceptional and concerned doctrinal arbitration or the application of the right of appeal.[33] One cannot overestimate the fact that the popes accepted this fully as compatible with that primacy of which they were so very conscious. Recently W. de Vries has pointed out the reason for the very important change in Rome's conception of the patriarchate, which occurred in the 13th century when the Latin patriarchates were set up.[34] This change is closely linked

---

[31] On this point, cf. H. Beck, *Theologie und geistliche Literatur im byzantinischen Reich* (Munich, 1959), pp. 60-97 and W. Hagemann, "Die rechtliche Stellung der Patriarchen von Alexandrien und Antiochien. Eine historische Untersuchung ausgehend von Kanon 6 von Nizäa," in *Ostkirchlichen Studien* (1964), pp. 171-91.

[32] For all this, see the noteworthy studies by W. de Vries, "Die Entstehung der Patriarchate des Ostens und ihr Verhältnis zur päpstlichen Vollgewalt," in *Scholastik* 37 (1962), and *Rom und die Patriarchate des Ostens* (Freiburg, 1963).

[33] The authenticity of some of these appeals has been called into question, even by Catholic historians. Cf. C. Vogel, "Unité et pluralité d'organisation ecclésiastique du IIIe au VIe siècle," in *L'Episcopat et l'Eglise universelle* (Paris, 1962), p. 634.

[34] Cf. W. de Vries, *loc. cit.,* pp. 359-65.

with the change in the notion of "metropolitan" that had taken
place in the West as a result of the extension of the granting of
the pallium, described above.

Canon 5 of the Fourth Lateran Council (1215) asserts:
"When the heads of these Churches have received the pallium
from the pope after taking the oath of allegiance and obedience,
they must confer the pallium on the bishops under their jurisdiction." Thus, by means of the pallium, patriarchal and other jurisdictions were considered as an emanation of, and participation in,
the *plenitudo potestatis* (the fullness of power) reserved exclusively to the pope. This, as we have seen, was already the case
in the West at that time. Michael Paleologus expressed this in
the proper terms in his confession of faith at the Council of
Lyons: "The *fullness of power* of the Roman Church consists in
that she admits the other Churches to a *share in her solicitude;*
this same Roman Church has honored many, and particularly
patriarchal, Churches with various privileges." [35]

Thus the patriarchs are assimilated to the Western archbishops of the later Middle Ages. In this way the third zone of the
East, in those parts in communion with Rome, developed toward that suburbicarian situation which marks the Uniat
Churches today. But this centralizing tendency, going beyond
historical contingencies, was linked as in the West with the views
of a "Roman school" inspired by the medieval papacy. It was
not the result of the teaching on the primacy, which remained
throughout the centuries wholly compatible with the existence of
three very differently organized zones within the universal
Church.

[35] Cf. the formula referred to in footnotes 15, 26 and 29.

August Franzen/*Freiburg, W. Germany*

The Council of Constance: Present State of the Problem

The Council of Constance occupies a unique place in theology and history. On the one hand, it has the great merit of having terminated the great Western Schism and of having restored the Church's long lost unity. On the other hand, it is laden with problems created by the conciliarism of its decrees *Haec sancta* and *Frequens,* by the thorny question of its canonical status, by the trial and execution of John Huss and by many other factors. Its very convocation was already controversial, and so were its composition, its organization, its voting procedure and its dealings at the election of Martin V. Compared with the usual type of council, it is in every way exceptional.

No wonder that its fascinating and difficult problems have always appealed to historians, canonists and theologians. In recent times the historian, Heinrich Finke of Freiburg,[1] together with his many disciples,[2] made an outstanding contribution to the history of the council by the publication of its *Acta* and detailed research. Thanks to him we are today well placed for the study of the outward events and troubled existence of the council insofar as sources are concerned. Unfortunately, we still lack

[1] I mention only one easily accessible edition of the proceedings: H. Finke, *Acta Concilii Constanciensis,* Vols. 1-4 (Münster, 1896-1928).

[2] Among them, J. Hollnsteiner, H. Heimpel and many others.

29

a satisfactory synthesis,[3] and this will remain impossible as long as we have no final assessment of the most important events and their connection, particularly of the way in which the already mentioned conciliarist decrees came about.

In the meantime some important preparatory work has been done in this field. After a passing phase of relative stagnation, research on the council during recent years shows again increased interest. On the occasion of the 550th anniversary of the council in 1964, the Theological Faculty of Freiburg in Breisgau published a "Festschrift" containing the papers read on that occasion and other essays.[4] This collection shows that the Council of Constance has become an astonishingly relevant topic today.

The first apparent impetus was provided by a seemingly unimportant event. The pope elected on October 28, 1958 chose the name John XXIII. The choice inevitably drew attention to that other John XXIII who summoned the Council of Constance in 1413 and solemnly opened it in the cathedral of Münster on November 5, 1414. By aligning himself with Pope John XXII (1316-1334) of Avignon, he rejected the popes of Pisa to whom the pope of the Council of Constance belonged. It was still not clear whether John XXIII's decision implied a pronouncement in favor of the exclusive legitimacy of the Roman popes from Urban VI to Gregory XII, or whether it meant to put aside the whole question of the papacy during the Schism and simply to continue as from 1378 on. For the moment it was significant that this clear decision against the legitimacy of the earlier John XXIII implied theological consequences. For, if the earlier John XXIII was not a legitimate pope, he could not legitimately summon a general council. Hence at least the first part of the Council of Constance could not be called ecumenical, and this in turn

---

[3] It is being prepared by K. Fink (Tübingen).

[4] *Festschrift: Das Konzil von Konstanz. Beiträge zu seiner Geschichte und Theologie,* commissioned by the Theological Faculty of the University of Freiburg and edited by A. Franzen and W. Müller (Freiburg, 1964), referred to as Franzen, *Konstanz; Konzil der Einheit. 500-Jahrfeier des Konzils von Konstanz* (Karlsruhe, 1964).

implied that the decree *Haec sancta,* published during this first period on April 6, 1415, could claim no dogmatic validity.

While historians were still discussing the bearing of these developments,[5] a second event occurred; it pointed even more urgently to the general and fundamental problems connected with Church councils: Vatican Council II was summoned on January 25, 1959. Since the pope made it quite clear that he wanted a change of direction in Church government, a break with the prevailing centralization and collegial co-responsibility of the bishops for the Church as a whole, the council was again entrusted with a vital function as the organ of the episcopal college. The convocation of the council also stimulated a new, intense interest in the general history of the councils,[6] leading to a closer theological examination of the role councils play in the Church.

Hans Küng reopened the discussion on the structures of the Church[7] and emphasized the collegial aspect of the cooperation between the pope and the episcopal college. Together with Paul de Vooght[8] he discerned a layer of sound, moderate, "conciliarist" thought behind extreme conciliarism, even in the Constance decrees *Haec sancta* and *Frequens.* Unexpectedly, theological and ecclesiological investigations focused on the Council of Constance. These two authors were joined by Hubert Jedin,[9]

[5] Cf. K. Fink, "Zur Beurteilung des grossen abendländischen Schismas," in *Zeitschr. f. Kirchengeschichte* 73 (1962), pp. 335ff.

[6] I mention the following: the collection *Le Concile et les Conciles,* with contributions from B. Botte, H. Marot, Y. Congar and others (Paris, 1960). Y. Congar. "Die Konzilien im Leben der Kirche," in *Una Sancta* 14 (1959), pp. 161ff.; H. Jedin, *Kleine Konziliengeschichte* (Freiburg, 1959); F. Dvornik, *The Ecumenical Councils* (New York, 1961); E. Iserloh, "Gestalt und Funktion der Konzilien in der Geschichte der Kirche," in *Festschrift für Bischof Wehr, Ekklesia* (Trier, 1962), pp. 149-69.

[7] H. Küng, *Strukturen der Kirche* (Quaestiones Disputatae 17) (Freiburg,[2] 1963); see also English edition, *idem, Structures of the Church* (New York: Nelson, 1963).

[8] P. de Vooght, "Der Konziliarismus bei den Konzilen von Konstanz und Basel," in *Das Konzil und die Konzile. Ein Beitrage zur Geschichte des Konzilsleben der Kirche* (Stuttgart, 1962), pp. 165-210. French: *Le Concile et les Conciles* (Paris, 1960), pp. 143-81.

[9] H. Jedin, *Bischöfliches Konzil oder Kirchenparlament? Ein Beitrag zur Ekklesiologie der Konzilien von Konstanz und Basel* (Basle, 1963).

Yves Congar[10] and others in an attempt to interpret the events and famous (or notorious) decrees of Constance. Congar compared the decrees with the definitions of Vatican Council I.[11] He came to the conclusion that both councils represented the two extremes of the swing of the pendulum: the "conciliarism" of Constance failed because it overemphasized the episcopal college at the expense of the papal primacy, while Vatican Council I overemphasized the primacy at the expense of the episcopal college. The situation therefore developed from an extreme conciliarism to a no less extreme papalism; now it had to strike the right balance.

In the meantime the opening of the council on October 11, 1962 set the ecclesiological discussion in full motion. John XXIII's idea of the collegial co-responsibility of the bishops prevailed, and eyes turned once again, beyond Vatican Council I, to the Council of Constance. Had the basic collegial structure of the Church not shown itself there as working in favor of the Church and the papacy? There is no doubt that the Council of Constance restored Church unity together with the Church's hierarchical structure. In Martin V it restored the primacy as the keystone of unity. Paradoxically, this papacy had landed itself in a schism merely by an exaggerated notion of itself and was incapable of overcoming by its own power the crisis at the top hierarchical level. The conciliar concept alone was able to save it and to restore unity. The one-eyed concentration on the danger of radical and revolutionary conciliarism, as it came to be formulated at the Council of Basle, blurred the view that a *moderate* conciliarism can contain sound elements, and that an "episcopalism", inspired by the spirit of true collegiality and linked with the pope, provides the primacy with a necessary complement and safeguard. The Council of Constance proved this.

In our day the primacy of the pope in the government of the Church is unquestioned and accepted by all Catholics, so that we

[10] Y. Congar, in *Das Konzil und die Konzile*, conclusion, pp. 331ff.
[11] *Ibid.*, pp. 384ff., in the contrast between *Papa* and *Ecclesia*. Cf. H. Küng, *op. cit.*, pp. 284ff.

can afford freely to discuss this problem. We are aware of the fact that the papacy and the college of bishops are called to guide the Church, not in opposition to each other but in unison. The basic collegial structure presupposes that Peter's primacy is personified in the pope as head of the episcopal college and that, on the other hand, the papacy does not hover unattached over the bishops and the Church. In working out this basic collegial structure of the Church "a look at the way in which the conciliar concept developed from Constance to Vatican Council I can only encourage the fathers of the present council to continue on the road they have taken".[12]

However difficult it may be to reconcile the conciliarist decrees of Constance with Vatican Council I's definitions of the primacy and infallibility of the pope, judging by the texts, we are today "in a better position to attempt a synthesis of Constance and Vatican Council I".[13] For "the Church of Vatican Council II feels strong enough . . . to tackle the genuine preoccupations that inspired the conciliarism of those days as it was supported by the best among the fathers of the Council of Constance".[14] "Secure in the possession of the teaching of Vatican Council I which underpinned the principle of the Church's unity, we can today, without fear of conciliarist or 'episcopalist' tendencies," bring out the idea of collegiality more forcefully. General councils and regional episcopal conferences have their own lawful place by the side of the pope's central power.

Theological discussion on the Council of Constance centers on that "conciliarism" contained in the decrees *Haec sancta* and *Frequens*. How must these decrees be understood and what is their theological significance? Can they claim full dogmatic validity in the same way as the doctrinal definitions of general councils? And if so, how do they fit in with the definitions of Vatican Council I? Two directly contradictory dogmatic truths are a theological impossibility. How can the contradiction be solved?

[12] F. König, "Die Konzilsidee von Konstanz bis Vatikanum II," in *Konzil der Einheit* (Karlsruhe, 1964), p. 30.
[13] *Ibid.*, p. 28.
[14] *Ibid.*, pp. 28f.

In his hermeneutic reflections on the decrees of the Council of Constance (*Hermeneutischen Überlegungen zu den Konstanzer Dekreten*),[15] Helmut Riedlinger has pointed out that the present state of canonical and historical research, the new ecclesiological approach and the discussions of Vatican Council II on primacy and episcopacy have led to a new situation in history and theology. This allows us better to understand and judge these decrees of the Council of Constance. Above all," our sense of the historicity and perspective of doctrinal statements has become much sharper", and it looks "as if today we are more prepared than at the beginning of the century to accept historical facts, even if they cut across current dogmatic theology and force us to qualify notions to which we were accustomed".[16] I want to indicate briefly some of these new approaches in history and theology.

I

THE QUESTION OF THE LEGALITY OF THE POPES AND OF THE COUNCIL OF CONSTANCE

When Pope John XXIII chose his name on October 28, 1958, he did not, of course, intend to give an authoritative decision on an historical controversy, nor does the mere fact of this choice do so. But it drew attention again to this problem. In fact, the question of legality is of quite decisive importance. Without it neither the Schism itself, nor the Councils of Pisa and Constance, nor the "conciliarism" of Constance, nor the decrees *Haec sancta* and *Frequens,* nor the proceedings at the election of Martin V, nor the conflict about the confirmation of the decrees can be understood. Even the unfortunate trial and execution of John Huss can be understood only against this background.

The background of the fateful double election of 1378 has recently been studied by various authors, particularly M. Seidl-

---

[15] Franzen, *op. cit.,* pp. 214-38.
[16] *Ibid.,* p. 214.

mayer,[17] W. Ullmann[18] and O. Přerovsky.[19] They all agree that
the cardinals' doubts and objections to the election of Urban
VI deserve more serious consideration than they have received
so far. It is a fact that the conclave in Rome, in 1378—the first
there after the exile of Avignon—took place under most tumul-
tuous circumstances. It is equally certain that the cardinals
elected Urban VI on April 8, 1378 under duress, even under
a threat to their lives. Hordes of armed Romans repeatedly
penetrated into the palace where the conclave was held, and on
the very morning of election day insisted with threats on the
election of a Roman. The French cardinals (11 of 16) saw
themselves forced to yield if they cared to leave the palace alive.
Immediately after the election they fled from Rome to safety.

Summoned by Urban, they returned to Rome soon after.
They took part in the coronation (April 18, 1378) and took
the usual oath on this occasion. For three months they could
not make up their minds, but finally the eleven French cardinals
and the one Spaniard (Peter of Luna, later Benedict XIII of
Avignon) left Rome again and in a manifesto sent to all Christendom on August 2, 1378 they declared that Urban's election
had been forced and was therefore illegal. On September 20,
1378 they elected the Frenchman Clement VII Pope, and he
again took up residence in Avignon. The three Italian cardinals
silently consented to these proceedings and later they, too, de-
serted Urban.

This rejection of Urban was no doubt influenced by political
and national intrigues, and even the selfish interests of the
worldly cardinals. Nevertheless, the basic fact at the start was
the actual election that had been seriously prejudiced by gen-

---

[17] M. Seidlmayer, *Die Anfänge des grossen abendländischen Schismas*
(Spanische Forschungen der Görres-Gesellschaft, II, 5) (Münster, 1940);
idem, in *Gesammelte Aufsätze zur Kulturgeschichte Spaniens,* IV, ed.
H. Finke (Münster, 1933).

[18] W. Ullmann, *The Origins of the Great Schism* (London, 1948).

[19] O. Přerovsky, *L'elezione di Urbano VI e l'insorgere dello scisma
d'occidente* (Miscellanea della società romana di storia patria, XX)
(Rome, 1960).

uine fear and the unjust use of force. The legitimacy of Urban's claims was, then as later, based on subsequent consent by the cardinals rather than on the actual election. This is still often the view today.[20] Yet, recent research has emphasized that neither the cardinals' participation in the coronation, nor their homage, nor their subsequent consent were unimpeded and voluntary. K. A. Fink, with his outstanding knowledge of the Vatican archives, has pointed out that "the material of the *Libri de schismate* in Rome has never yet been exhausted" and has drawn attention to "the legal documents and factors that led to the composition of these books, and the secret letters and messages of the cardinals that weakened or invalidated their official position".[21] This rules out any further question of their free and full consent. Immediately after their rejection of Urban the cardinals themselves declared that they had no intention of rectifying the election. This could be done only by a completely new election of Urban.

Přerovsky has proven that the cardinals had still another objection to the validity of the election of Urban, namely their doubt whether the pope was mentally responsible. An unsuspected eyewitness and German member of Urban's court, Dietrich von Niem, has reported on the impression that Urban's domineering, fanatical and overweening behavior made on the cardinals immediately after his election: they believed that they had elected someone who was mentally unbalanced. The sudden elevation to papal dignity seemed to have gone to his head.[22] The fact that later on his own cardinals whom he had himself

---

[20] Thus, for instance, J. Villiger, *Lex. Theol. u. Kirche* I, (2nd ed., 1957), p. 22; both L. von Pastor, *Papstgeschichte* Vol. 1 (12th ed., 1955), pp. 125ff., and A. Hauck, *Kirchengeschichte Deutschlands*, Vol. 2 (1953), p. 676, wholly accepted the subsequent tacit consent given at Urban's coronation and that therefore the cardinals had definitely forfeited their right to protest against the legal irregularities at the election. For the whole problem see A. Franzen, "Zur Vorgeschichte des Konstanzer Konzils," in Franzen, *Konstanz,* pp. 3-35.

[21] K. Fink, "Zur Beurteilung des . . . Schismas," in *Zeitschr. f. Kirchengeschichte* 73 (1962), p. 338.

[22] On this point, see also L. von Pastor, *op. cit.,* p. 129, footnote 3.

created wanted to put him in the charge of a guardian shows
that his own supporters and close collaborators doubted his
responsibility.[23] History still looks on him as more or less mentally deranged.[24]

Final clarity on the degree of his insanity and on the fear
and coercion to which the cardinals were subjected at the election will never be reached. We have to be content with the judgment that "the election of Urban VI was neither absolutely
valid nor absolutely invalid, and that contemporaries, including those most immediately concerned in the events, were in a
state of invincible ignorance".[25] But, according to canon law, the
election of a person of unsound mind is illegal.

In any case, the cardinals thought they were justified in
proceeding to a new election, and even felt it a duty. Whatever
other motives they may have had do not concern us here. Ob-
jectively speaking, I simply state the fact that the state of affairs
showed there was uncertainty about the election. But *if* it is
not certain that Urban VI was unquestionably the legitimate
pope, it follows that Clement VII was not unquestionably an
illegitimate pope. Hence, after the election of Clement on September 20, 1378, there were in fact two doubtful popes. The
doubt cannot simply be set aside; it was an "invincible error"
for the contemporaries as for us today.

We must face this fact unemotionally in order to understand
how the split persisted with such obstinacy for decades. Both
lines of papal successors were honestly convinced of the legitimacy of their position and believed they had to fight for the
genuine apostolic succession and the stability of the Church,
and so they rejected the claim of the opposition and fought for
their own to the last ditch. Nobody could understand the posi-

---

[23] *Ibid.*, p. 146.

[24] See, for example, the various judgments of him in F. Seppelt and
G. Schwaiger, *Das Papsttum im Spätmittelalter*, Vol. 4 (1957), p. 205;
K. Bihlmeyer and H. Tüchle, *Kirchengeschichte*, Vol. 2 (1948), p. 384,
(English edition, *Church History*, Vol. 2 (Westminster, Md.: Newman
Press).

[25] K. Fink, *loc. cit.*, p. 338.

tion any more. When there had been double elections and schisms the matter had in former times been finally decided by the prevailing opinion (*sensus communis*) or some great saint like Bernard of Clairvaux who settled the papal schism of 1130,[26] but in 1378 both these routes were closed. Important contemporary saints were found on both sides: Catherine of Siena supported Urban VI; St. Vincent Ferrer supported Clement VII. And nothing shows better the need for caution in distributing the blame for the situation than the fact that the austere and incorruptible penitential preacher St. Vincent was for many years the confessor of Clement's successor, the Spaniard Benedict XIII (1394-1417, d. 1424), in Avignon. If he had had the slightest doubt about the legitimacy of the popes of Avignon, he would have been unable to answer before God and his conscience for his unstinted support of Clement and Benedict. The same holds for Catherine on the other side.

It is, therefore, impossible to distribute the blame between the popes. Their contemporaries already saw this. While at the start, for example, both Catherine and Vincent fiercely attacked the pope and cardinals of the opposite party, accusing them of having created the schism, this attitude was abandoned later on and people merely concentrated on finding ways and means of ending the schism.

Of the three ways suggested by the University of Paris in 1394 to overcome the schism, two appealed to the goodwill of the popes themselves (*via cessionis:* yielding, and *via compromissi,* compromise) and only the third way (*via concilii,* through a council) tried it without this appeal, more or less as a last resort. It was no longer a question of "deciding" the controversial papal election of 1378, but only of making the way free for a restoration of the Church's unity. Only when it became obvious after a long period of patient waiting that the popes themselves were unable to find a way of overcoming the tragic split, based on

[26] F. Schmale, *Studien zum Schisma des Jahres 1130. Abhandlungen zur kirchlichen Rechtsgeschichte,* Vol. 3 (Cologne, 1960).

the situation itself or on their sense of personal responsibility,[27] did the *via concilii* begin to gain ground. For example, John Gerson, who at the start had been constantly opposed to the conciliar solution, began to favor it in 1408. Only then did the call for a council become universal as the last means of saving the situation.[28]

When the thirteen cardinals of both groups finally decided at Leghorn on March 25, 1409 to summon a general council at Pisa in order to overcome the schism, they did not want this council to decide the question of legitimacy, nor to make "conciliarist" statements on the council's superiority over the papacy; they merely intended to put aside the two controversial popes whose position had been hardened by the duration of the schism and so to open the way for a single new pope. The Council of Pisa (1409), therefore, was mainly a trial of two deficient popes who had offended the papacy and the Church's unity by persistently encouraging the state of schism, and so had become heretics. Both popes, Gregory XII and Benedict XIII, were accused, at the fifteenth session on June 5, 1409, of heretical conduct toward the dogma of the "one holy . . . Church" and deposed. While still at Pisa, the cardinals then elected a new pope, Alexander V, on June 26, 1409.[29]

H. Zimmermann has recently published several studies[30] in

[27] G. Posthumus Meyjes, *Jean Gerson. Zijn Kerkpolitiek en Ecclesiologie* (The Hague, 1963), pp. 313ff., thinks that the popes could at most be blamed for acting on the higher, not personal, motive of being utterly bound to a traditional doctrinal system.

[28] Fliche-Martin, XIV, *L'Eglise au temps du Grand Schisme et de la crise conciliaire, 1378-1449* (Tours, 1962), pp. 139ff.

[29] For the Council of Pisa, cf. J. Vincke, "Acta Concilii Pisani," in *Röm. Quartalschrift* 46 (1938), pp. 81-331; *idem, Briefe zum Pisaner Konzil* (Bonn, 1940); *idem, Schriftstücke zum Pisaner Konzil* (Bonn, 1942); A. Brüggen, *Die Predigten des Pisaner Konzils* (Theol. diss. in typescript, Freiburg, 1963).

[30] H. Zimmermann, "Papstabsetzungen des Mittelalters," in *Mitt. d. Inst. f. Oesterreichische Gesch. forschung* (MIOG) 69 (1961), pp. 1-84 and 241-91; 70 (1962), pp. 60-110; 68 (1960), pp. 209-25; 72 (1964), pp. 74-109 (Ergebnisse, Folgerungen und Nachwirkungen), *idem Oesterreichisches Archiv f. Kirchenrecht* 12 (1961), pp. 207-30; *idem,* "Die Absetzung der Päpste auf den Konstanzer Konzil. Theorie und Praxis," in Franzen, *Konstanz,* pp. 113-37.

which he investigated the procedure and canonical principles used during the Middle Ages when popes were deposed. In spite of the general acceptance of the canonical principle of the immunity of the "first See" (*Prima sedes a nemine iudicatur*),[31] he has shown that the old canon law allowed for exceptions. Apostasy in particular constituted a ground for deposing a pope. "In that case it was not a true pope and occupant of the first See who was tried but an impious usurper of the *Cathedra Petri* and a wanton intruder into the Roman Church." [32] The heresy clause, which goes back to the condemnation of Pope Honorius by the sixth ecumenical Council of Constantinople (681), had been officially accepted by the papacy since Hadrian II (867-872) as Zimmermann proves, and from that time on was applied as "the fully authoritative norm in the case of depositions of popes".[33] Cardinal Humbert of Silva Candida gave it its final formula (*nisi deprehendatur a fide devius:* unless he is found to deviate from the faith) in the 11th century, and toward the end of that century it appears for the first time in the canonical collection of Cardinal Deusdedit. Through Ivo of Chartres[34] and Gratian[35] it became commonly accepted as part of canon law. The concept of heresy took on a much wider meaning than it has today and included any notorious scandal affecting the Church as a whole.

It is significant that a very careful distinction was made be-

---

[31] Zimmermann shows that this juridical formula arose out of the so-called forgeries of Symmachus, between 498 and 506, in *MIOG* 69 (1961), pp. 2ff.

[32] *Idem, MIOG* 72 (1964), p. 77.

[33] *Ibid.*, p. 79.

[34] *Ibid.*, p. 77; Ivo of Chartres, Decretum V, 23, in *P. L.* 161, col. 330; R. Sprandel, *Ivo von Chartres und seine Stellung in der Kirchengeschichte* (1962); for Deusdedit, see V. von Glanwell, *Die Kanonessammlung des Kardinals Deusdedit* (1905), p. 178.

[35] *Decretum Gratiani*, c.6, D.XL, ed. A. Friedberg, Vol. 1, p. 146: "If the pope, neglectful of his own and his brethren's salvation, is proved useless and remiss in his duties, and moreover drags innumerable people down with him, horde-like, away from the good, he will suffer many afflictions in the slavery of hell for all eternity. Let no mortal presume to argue his guilt, since, though he judges all, he is not to be judged by anyone unless he deviates from the faith."

tween the person and the office of the pope. The accusation and condemnation of a heretical pope was in no way directed against the papacy as an institution, but merely rid both papacy and Church of a wicked intruder who in fact did not legitimately occupy the first See. He therefore stood trial merely as a pseudo-pope and it was concluded that the papal See was vacant and should be filled again.

How deeply this opinion was rooted in the whole medieval canon law has become evident through numerous recent studies. W. Ullmann,[36] B. Tierney,[37] L. Buisson,[38] J. M. Moynihan,[39] M. Wilks,[40] W. Kölmel [41] and others all agree that both rigid papalist canonists and the so-called conciliarists held that the principle of papal immunity allowed for exceptions (simony, heresy, etc.) and that in these exceptional cases a given institution was entitled to correct the pope and if necessary to depose him. This right belongs either to the college of cardinals or the general council. The initiative lies here with the cardinals as the electors of the pope and his most important collaborators in the government of the Church; but it is up to the council to give its decision on the accusations and to pronounce judgment on the pseudo-pope.

If we keep in mind this judicial situation, accepted by ancient

[36] W. Ullmann, *Die Machtstellung des Papsttums im Mittelalter* (Gratz, 1960). In connection with this, see F. Kempf, "Die papstliche Gewalt in der mittelalterlichen Welt," in *Saggi storici intorno al Papato* (Rome, 1959), pp. 117-69.

[37] B. Tierney, *Foundations of Conciliar Theory. The Contribution of the Medieval Canonists from Gratian to the Great Schism* (Cambridge, 1955); idem, "Pope and Council," in *Mediaeval Studies* 19 (1957), pp. 197-218.

[38] L. Buisson, *Potestas und Caritas. Die päpstliche Gewalt im Spätmittelalter* (Cologne, 1959), and the review of this book by B. Panzram, in *Theologische Revue* 59 (1963), pp. 112-8.

[39] J. Moynihan, "Papal Immunity and Liability in the Writings of the Medieval Canonists," in *Analecta Gregoriana* 120 (Rome, 1961).

[40] M. Wilks, *The Problem of Sovereignty in the Later Middle Ages. The Papal Monarchy with Augustinus Triumphus and the Publicists* (Cambridge, 1963).

[41] W. Kölmel, "Einheit und Zweiheit der Gewalt im Corpus Mysticum. Zur Souveränitätslehre des Augustinus Triumphus," in *Hist. Jahrbuch der Görres-Gesellschaft* 82 (1963), pp. 103-47.

canonical tradition, we cannot doubt that the procedure of the Council of Pisa, summoned by the cardinals, stood up in law. At this council 24 cardinals, 200 bishops from all over the world, 287 abbots and superiors-general of other religious orders, about 100 chapters and 13 universities with about 700 Masters of Theology and Canon Law, and most European princes were represented. During the eighth session, on May 10, 1409, the council declared itself to be canonically constituted and to be a general council; by far the greatest part of Christendom considered it valid. The pope elected by the Council, Alexander V, who solemnly closed it on August 7, 1409, was accepted, yet the council still could not maintain itself in the long run. Gregory XII and Benedict XIII clung to their position and "out of the nefarious twofold conflict" arose that "threefold conflict, cursed by all". According to the unanimous conclusion reached by recent research, this was due to Alexander's successor, John XXIII (1410-1415, d. 1419) whose evil life and behavior endangered both the council and his own legitimate position.

J. Vincke, editor of the *Acta* of the Council of Pisa, also examined this problem[42] and concluded that, in spite of the opposition of the Roman Pope, Gregory XII, and the one of Avignon, Benedict XIII, "the papal succession of Pisa would probably have succeeded as the legitimate one if John XXIII had not ruined its reputation".[43] A. Brüggen reaches the same conclusion: "If the Popes of Pisa were afterward considered anti-popes, the reason seems to be that the second Pope of Pisa, John XXIII, showed such unworthy behavior that he dragged his predecessor and the whole Council of Pisa with him in his own catastrophic fall",[44] and K. A. Fink sums up: "If we take the results of recent research seriously, we can no longer designate the synod of Pisa as a *conciliabulum* (a pretended coun-

[42] Cf. footnote 29. See also J. Vincke, "Zu den Konzilien von Perpignan und Pisa," in *Röm. Quartalschrift* 50 (1955), pp. 89-94.

[43] *Idem, Lexikon für Theologie und Kirche* Vol. 8 (2nd ed., 1963), p. 521.

[44] A. Brüggen, *op. cit.*, p. 129.

cil)".[45] At all events, it seems certain that by far the greatest part of Christendom maintained the legitimacy of the Council of Pisa and its popes, with the exception of the small groups that had coagulated around Gregory XII and Benedict XIII. Only "later the question of the ecumenical character of the council and the legitimacy of Alexander V was dealt with, often adversely, but never finally settled (not even in the list of popes in the *Annuario Pontificio* since 1947)".[46]

When, therefore, John XXIII called the Council of Constance in 1413 and opened it in November, 1414, he acted as a legitimate and generally accepted pope. Both these actions were legal, and the Council of Constance stands, therefore, as ecumenical from the start. It is true that in the meantime John's prestige had seriously declined through his own fault, soon resulting in the loss of the domination he had enjoyed at the beginning of the council. He was deposed, not because people doubted his legitimacy, but because they objected to his simoniacal intrigues at his election, his immorality, his faithless utterances and his irreligious conduct. His opposition to the reunion efforts of the council and particularly his flight from Constance (March 20-21, 1415), which looked like an attack on the synod, put him, moreover, in the position of a schismatic and heretic. H. Zimmermann has shown recently that his trial and subsequent deposition (May 29, 1415) were conducted throughout according to canonical rules and usage.[47]

But did the council not somehow accept and respect the legitimacy of the Roman Pope Gregory XII? It is known that the council admitted that he belatedly consented to its convocation in his own name before he resigned voluntarily. The Roman group saw therein a confirmation of his legitimacy and considered the council ecumenical from the moment of Gregory's convocation.

The council had to settle the question whether Gregory should

---

[45] K. Fink, *loc. cit.,* p. 339.
[46] J. Vincke, *loc. cit.,* p. 521.
[47] H. Zimmermann, "Die Absetzung der Päpste auf dem Konstanzer Konzil," in Franzen, *Konstanz,* pp. 113-37, esp. 126ff.

be treated as pope. It arose from the practical problem of how to receive Gregory's delegate, Cardinal Dominici: should he be treated as a private Christian or as an official papal delegate? [48] John XXIII and his supporters, who were still a majority in November and December 1414, refused him the honors due to the one true papal delegate. Cardinal d'Ailly, however, insisted that Dominici should be treated honorably, and suggested at the same time that if Benedict XIII also sent a delegate, he would be treated with the same honor. Later the Emperor and many others agreed with him. But this was not done because the claims of Gregory and Benedict were recognized as legitimate, but because it was hoped that this might ease the effort of achieving unity once more. As, moreover, Gregory had already offered to resign voluntarily and the council could afford not to use any violent action, it allowed him on July 4, 1415 in Constance "contrary to the true facts of the situation to stage a reconstitution of the synod by a bull read aloud by Cardinal Dominici in the name of Gregory XII".[49] Apart from Gregory and his supporters, the sources clearly show that no one in Constance took this seriously.[50]

According to the present state of research, therefore, it is no longer possible to consider this belated "convocation" by Gregory as constituting the ecumenical Council of Constance. The legitimacy of the popes of both Rome and Avignon had been clearly rejected, not only by the questionable double election of 1378 and a schism which lasted for several decades, but also by the canonical deposition of 1409. Those who took part in the Council of Constance did not dream of recognizing either of them again. Nor was this necessary for the constitution of the council at this moment because it was not until April 6 that the

[48] On this point see A. Franzen, "Das Konzil der Einheit. Einigungsbemühungen und konziliare Gedanken auf dem Konstanzer Konzil. Die Dekrete *Haec sancta und Frequens,*" in *Konstanz,* pp. 69-112, esp. "Die erste Phase des Konstanzer Konzils," pp. 77 ff.

[49] H. Zimmermann, *loc. cit.,* p. 128.

[50] For this fourteenth general session, cf. Mansi, XXVII, pp. 730ff.; see also J. Hollerbach, "Die gregorianische Partei, Sigismund und das Konstanzer Konzil," in *Röm. Quartalschrift* 23 (1909), pp. 34ff.

assembly designated itself as "lawfully gathered together in the Holy Spirit and constituting a general council" in the decree *Haec sancta,* and so constituted itself an ecumenical synod.

How little importance the council attached to Gregory's "convocation" can be seen in the fact that it offered Benedict XIII the same right of convocation. The council was not concerned with reopening the legitimacy question, nor did it seek any legitimization and authorization from popes it did not recognize; it merely tried to secure the cooperation of the popes and their groups with the council. Indeed, if they did not want to see a repetition of the failure of Pisa, they had to secure the broadest possible basis for the restoration of unity. The general council's own legitimacy lay in the fact that the whole Church took part and recognized it. When the groups were won over, it would be possible to proceed more forcefully against an individual pope, as happened with Benedict,[51] as soon as he had lost his support (Treaty of Perpignan, Autumn 1415).

II

THE CONCILIARISM OF CONSTANCE
AND THE DECREES *Haec Sancta* AND *Frequens*

With the summoning of the Councils of Pisa (1409) and Constance (1414) the road to a conciliar solution (*via concilii*) had been taken. But did this already imply "conciliarism"?

P. de Vooght maintains that at Constance "the prevailing opinion was conciliarist".[52] H. Küng expressed himself more cautiously when he said that "during the Great Schism (and beyond it) conciliar ideas were advocated everywhere throughout the Church";[53] for this he refers to the brilliant study of Tierney, and his witnesses are: for Germany, Konrad von Gelnhausen, Heinrich von Langenstein and Dietrich von Niem; for France, Pierre d'Ailly and John Gerson; for Spain, Andreas

---

[51] H. Zimmermann, *loc. cit.,* pp. 129ff.
[52] P. de Vooght, in *Das Konzil und die Konzile, op. cit.,* p. 168.
[53] H. Küng, *op. cit.,* p. 265.

Randulf, and for Italy, Francesco Zabarella. It would have been better if he had first very carefully distinguished between "conciliarist" and "conciliar". "Conciliarism" usually means that in principle the council is above the pope; its most extreme form was developed by Marsilio of Padua and William of Ockham. One cannot say that this teaching was already universally advocated during the Great Schism. On the contrary, it was rarely asserted, and then in an attenuated form, until it developed more radically at Constance and particularly at Basle.

The basic mistake of older scholars, such as Kneer, Hirsch and Wenck, was to dub all "conciliar" ideas as "conciliarist" when they were concerned with the place of the council and with granting the council a controlling function over the person, but not the office, of the pope in some well-known exceptional cases. This was in turn derived from Marsilio. More recent studies have corrected this error by discovering these "conciliar" elements in the study of canon law and "in the totally orthodox and traditional ecclesiology of the 12th and 13th centuries" (Küng). But they have also shown what a basic difference there is between these traditional elements and the wholly new, heretical, conciliarist ideas of Marsilio. It is misunderstanding the work of Ullmann, Kuttner and Tierney[54] to conclude from it that the medieval canonists of the 12th and 13th centuries already had "conciliarist" notions which were only later developed heretically. The truth is rather that the typically "conciliarist" elements were indeed new, heretical and derived from Marsilio, as the older scholars had rightly pointed out. There were however other elements in the older teaching of canon law which were often similar to the new elements, thus providing a starting point for the conciliarism of Marsilio and Ockham. The ambivalent notion of "conciliarism" has misled many, and still hampers us today in the understanding of the Constance decrees.

Apart from the work of Tierney, the studies of H. Zimmermann have thrown considerable light on the inner transition

---

[54] Cf. the studies already mentioned of Ullmann, Tierney, Buisson, Moynihan, Wilks, Kölmel and others.

from conciliar to conciliarist thought. The problem is best understood when seen in the context of the numerous depositions of popes during the Middle Ages. In this way we can broadly outline the present state of research as follows:

1. The broad canonical tradition that the first See is beyond judgment goes back to the early Middle Ages; at the same time it includes the rules for dealing with the personal defection of a pope in the so-called heresy clause. On the one hand, the powerful impetus given to papal primacy since the Gregorian Reform (*Dictatus papae,* 1075) reinforced the idea of the immunity and dignity of the papacy. It found its practical realization in Innocent III and Boniface VIII. But its theoretical elaboration was developed only by the canon lawyers of the curia in the 14th century—at a time, therefore, when papal supremacy had collapsed. Aegidius Romanus (d. 1316), on whose writings Boniface VIII based his bull *Unam sanctam,* developed the image of the pope's unique fullness of power and his special position, according to which all power in the Church is founded in the papacy.[55] Augustinus Triumphus (d. 1328) interpreted the pope's plenitude of power as derived immediately from divine power,[56] and Alvarus Pelagius (d. 1349) attributed to the pope alone more power than to the rest of the Church and the councils "apart from him" (*seorsum*).[57] All exaggerations aside, the decisive factor is that pope and Church are no longer seen as a unity, but appear to stand in contrast, to be detached, so that in general they can be treated "apart" (*seorsum*). To understand this development one should remember that, in spite

---

[55] Aegidius Romanus, *De ecclesiae potestate* III, 9 (ed. R. Scholz, Weimar, 1929; new impr. 1961): "All that the Church can do is contained in the supreme pontiff" (*Totum posse quod est in Ecclesia reservatur in summo pontifice*). Cf. M. Wilks, *op. cit.,* p. 35, n. 3.

[56] Augustinus Triumphus, *Summa de potestate ecclesiastica,* q.6, a.1; M. Wilks, *op. cit.,* p. 374, n. 1.

[57] Alvarus Pelagius, *De planctu ecclesiae* I, 6: "*Plus potest Papa solus . . . quam tota ecclesia catholica et concilia seorsum*" (The pope alone has more power . . . than the whole Catholic Church and the councils apart from him).

of its new supremacy, the papacy was threatened on many sides; the theoretical threat lay in the heresy clause that might be interpreted lightheartedly or maliciously.

On the other hand, M. Wilks[58] has convincingly proved, with a wealth of evidence from original sources, how even the rigid canonists of the curia maintained the tradition of the heresy clause, and built it into their system. It is, therefore, clear that according to the general and accepted teaching of the Church at the time, a pope could be deposed from the Chair of Peter if he was personally guilty of heresy. It is also clear that there had to be some group capable of deciding such a case. The only bodies available during the later Middle Ages were the college of cardinals and the council. Centrally placed as electors of the pope and his collaborators in the government of the Church, the cardinals had a certain predominance; this consisted not so much in that they could exclude the council but rather in that they had a certain right of initiative: it was up to them, in the first place, to call and guide the council to decide on the pope's heresy and to give its verdict. This already implied a prejudgment that might easily develop into a certain control over the pope. Nevertheless, the final judgment rested with the council.

Since the Emperor had, on the whole, lost his position as protector of the Church, and autocratic depositions of popes by the Emperor (as at Sutri in 1046) had become impossible, he, too, could do nothing else but turn to a general council to present his complaints against a pope. These complaints became more and more customary after Frederick II (1239-40). The cardinals of the Colonna family appealed to a general council against Boniface VIII, and soon afterward Philip the Fair of France, and a little later Emperor Lewis the Bavarian, appealed against John XXII. This appeal to the council became a favorite weapon against popes who had made themselves unpopular. Such action was still directed exclusively against an individual person, not against the institution of the papacy.

[58] M. Wilks, *op. cit.*, pp. 479ff.

2. The conflict turned to a fight against the institution only with Marsilio of Padua; this put the problem on another level and turned it in the direction of heterodox conciliarism.

Marsilio wrote his *Defensor Pacis* in Paris in 1324[59] and fled two years later to Lewis the Bavarian to whom he gave legal advice in his fight against the pope from then on.[60] The new element in his democratic conception of the Church, based on Aristotle's political teaching,[61] consisted in a radical break with the hierarchical structure of the Church and the overthrow of the whole ecclesiastical organization bound up with it. The Church is the community of the faithful. There is no essential distinction between clergy and laity. All the faithful can take part in a general council. Those that have a spiritual office have no privilege in the voting on matters of faith nor in other decisions. Since the council as a whole derives its authority from the People of God, every participant can act and decide only as representative and mandatory of the faithful by whom he is delegated. The pope, too, is only the representative of the congregation of the faithful and holds the executive office of the general council. Legislation belongs to the people, or to the council as representing the people. The pope has executive power only. Subordinate to the council, he owes it obedience and can be deposed at any time.

The elimination of the hierarchical order and the democrati-

---

[59] Cf. H. Segall, *Der Defensor Pacis des Marsilius von Padua. Grundfragen der Interpretation* (Vienna, 1959); see the observations by S. Krüger in *Hist. Zeitschrift* 193 (1961), pp. 660f. There is an English edition of the *Defensor Pacis,* produced by C. W. Prévité-Orton (Cambridge, 1928).

[60] For his political activity at the court of the German Emperor, cf. C. Müller, *Der Kampf Ludwigs d. Bayern mit der röm. Curie* (I-II, 1870-1880) and A. Hauck, *Kirchengeschichte Deutschlands,* Vol. 1 (1954), pp. 485ff.

[61] For the question of his Aristotelianism, see M. Grignaschi, "Le rôle de l'Aristotélisme dans le *Defensor Pacis,*" in *Revue d'Histoire et de Philosophie religieuses* 25 (1955), pp. 301-48; for a recently discovered commentary by Marsilio on the *Metaphysics,* see H. Riedlinger in *Bulletin de la société Intern. pour l'Etude de la Philosophie Médiévale* 4 (Louvain, 1962).

zation of the Church implied in Marsilio's system were ideas so foreign to the tradition of the Western Church and so revolutionary that they progressed very slowly. The fact that John XXII condemned solemnly some of the theses in 1327 and stigmatized the author as a dangerous heretic had some effect. If William of Ockham had not adopted Marsilio's ideas and incorporated them in his *Dialogus,* they might have petered out. But with Ockham's nominalism they made their way into contemporary thought, and finally, though only in the 15th century, they became fully active at the time of the Council of Basle.

3. The Great Schism made it obviously easier for Marsilio's thought to penetrate into the broad stream of canonical tradition. But today we know that it was accepted only with great hesitation and rather late, as can be seen in the authors mentioned above. For, if Konrad von Gelnhausen, Heinrich von Langenstein, Pierre d'Ailly and John Gerson were previously mentioned easily in the same breath with Marsilio and Ockham as the fathers of the real "conciliarism", recent research has shown that these personalities were anything but revolutionary and subversive. The work of P. Meyjes is particularly revealing on this point. He shows that, particularly on the issue of the elimination of the hierarchical structure and the democratization of the Church, Langenstein and Gelnhausen did not follow Marsilio and Ockham, and even firmly rejected their ideas. Of Gelnhausen's famous *Epistola concordiae* (May, 1380), which has been called "the first scientific presentation of conciliarism", the author says in his conclusion: "Above all, it seems to us that the *Epistola concordiae* must be interpreted in a conservative sense".[62]

The same holds for d'Ailly (1352-1420)[63] and Gerson (1363-

---

[62] G. Posthumus Meyjes, *op. cit.,* p. 291.

[63] Apart from the older monographies of P. Tschackert (Gotha, 1877) and L. Salembier (1886; Tourcoing, 1931), the following deserve mention: J. P. McGowan, *P. d'Ailly and the Council of Constance* (Washington, 1936); M. Lieberman, "Gerson et d'Ailly," in *Romania* 78 (Paris, 1957), pp. 433-62; 79 (1958), pp. 339-75; 80 (1959), pp. 289-

1429)[64] in the period including the Council of Constance where they played a major part. To call them simply "conciliarists", as is still done today,[65] is misleading. Meyjes has proved that Gerson kept consciously and rather nervously aloof from Marsilio, whom he called a heretic, and whose "conciliarist" political ideas he rejected, so that "it is out of the question that Gerson was influenced by Marsilio".[66] There is not a single quotation of Marsilio or Ockham in d'Ailly's basic treatise *De Materia Concilii Generalis* (1402), but the cardinal frequently refers to established canonists and he remains wholly within the framework of the Church's tradition.[67] This is the more significant as both d'Ailly and Gerson accepted Ockham's philosophy throughout and represented the nominalistic *via moderna* in their teaching and their writings. They were well acquainted with Ockham's *Dialogus,* but rejected his political ideas on Church and State.

It is interesting to follow the development of d'Ailly and Gerson during the schism. During the first decades both appear to be staunch conservatives,[68] firmly upholding the rights of the papacy and proposing the easiest course for the popes during the negotiations. They think that only the *via cessionis* or the *via compromissi* can lead to results. The popes themselves should take the road to unity and should either resign voluntarily or one should withdraw in favor of the other, their main

---

336; 81 (1960), pp. 44-98; B. Meller, *Studien zur Erkenntnislehre des Peter von Ailly* (Freiburg, 1954) which contains the text of d'Ailly's *Tractatus de materia concilii generalis* (1402) on pp. 289-336.

[64] J. Morrall, *Gerson and the Great Schism* (Manchester, 1960); Z. Rueger, "Le *De auctoritate concilii* de Gerson," in *Revue d'histoire Ecclésiastique* 53 (1958), pp. 775-95. Cp. Posthumus Meyjes, *op. cit.,* and A. Franzen, "Zur Vorgeschichte des Konstanzer Konzils," in Franzen, *Konstanz,* pp. 20-9.

[65] M. Pacaut, *La théocratie. L'église et le pouvoir au moyen âge* (Paris, 1957), pp. 200ff.; P. de Vooght, in *Das Konzil und die Konzile, op. cit.,* p. 166.

[66] Posthumus Meyjes, *op. cit.,* p. 283.

[67] He takes his definition of the council from the Decretists Huguccio and Bartholomew of Brescia, to whom he refers explicitly. Cf. *Tractatus de materia concilii,* ed. Meller, *op. cit.,* p. 300.

[68] Cf. my study in *Konstanz,* pp. 21ff.

preoccupation being to save papal authority. Gerson, in particular, firmly maintained the divine institution of the hierarchy and derived the primacy immediately from Christ. Against Heinrich von Langenstein he emphasized that this primacy was bound up with the office of Peter in the See of Rome through Christ's will and institution.[69] Papal primacy, the Roman Church and the universal Church are one; the primacy is linked with the See of Rome for the government of the Church.

How these and other propositions can be called "conciliarist" defies comprehension. Both Gerson and d'Ailly shelved for a long time even the usual "conciliar" notions. Only when decades of fruitless negotiation had clearly shown that the two popes were incapable of solving the crisis of the primacy and there was a genuine threat to the organization of the Church, did they change their mind. After 1408 they, too, agreed that the *via concilii* was the only way out of the impasse, when the last attempts to restore union had failed. Until then they had no time for a conciliar solution, according to Meyjes.

The call for a general council which would do away with the schism became ever louder from about 1404-1406 onward. It is, however, not yet in any way characterized by "conciliarism" but is altogether traditional in spirit. The sermons preached at the Council of Pisa[70] give clear evidence of the anxious desire to follow procedures which time-honored canon law provided for certain emergencies. The intention was to remove those popes, who for some reason could not be upheld, in order to clear the way for the papacy. The actions of the Council of Pisa cannot be construed in a conciliaristic sense but only as wholly conservative.

The same can be said of Constance, though with some qualifications. During the interval since Pisa, confidence in the papacy had sunk to a very low level. The time was ripe for more radical solutions; some effective action was necessary to put an end to the misery of the schism, and only the council could still help.

---

[69] Posthumus Meyjes, *op. cit.*, p. 293.
[70] A. Brüggen, *op. cit.*

But the very way in which Pope John XXIII was allowed to call and to open the council shows already that the old custom was maintained and that there was no intention of turning it into a "conciliarist" council, in the sense of Marsilio of Padua. During November and December 1414 the pope's position was unquestioned. Then came the conflict primarily concerned with the person of John XXIII. It grew clear that, in order to open the way to unity, all three papal claimants had to be deposed. Emperor Sigismund seems to have had this idea from the start for he had already made contact with the other two popes of Rome and Avignon.

In order to defend his position John claimed that he had been elected as the one and only legitimate pope by the general Council of Pisa. An ecumenical council could not err and its decisions must in any case be respected: they were irrevocable. To this d'Ailly replied that only the universal Church was infallible, and that an individual council could issue decrees that were wrong and could be revoked, "because, according to some great theologians, a general council not only can err in fact, but also in law and, what is more, in matters of faith".[71] Insofar as his principal concern was to show that the decision of Pisa on the legitimacy question of the popes was no infallible doctrinal decision, he was right. But he went further and, referring to "certain great theologians", he denied in general that a general council was infallible in matters of faith. Who were these authorities whom he did not name? Here one can clearly see the influence of Ockham, Marsilio and Langenstein. A doctrinal decision does not derive its final certainty from the council but from the subsequent acceptance by the universal Church. This was an assertion of far-reaching significance.

To John's claim that he alone had summoned the council and that therefore he alone was in control, d'Ailly replied by pointing to the function of the Emperor in charge of the council by virtue of his office of *Advocatus Ecclesiae,* as Constantine the

---

[71] H. von der Hardt, *Magnum oecumenicum Constantiense Concilium,* *II* (Frankfurt-Leipzig, 1697-1700), p. 201.

Great had been in the past. Similar views on the position of the Emperor had once been propounded by Marsilio, although, no doubt, as a matter of basic principle. D'Ailly used this argument only to get around a concrete difficulty here and now; later on he no longer interpreted the Emperor's position in this fashion.

John fled from Constance (March 20-21, 1415) when they began to accuse him of immoral behavior and he began to realize that his position had become untenable. From Schaffhausen he bombarded the council with objections. His plan was to cut the ground from under the council fathers' feet and so to force a dissolution. But thanks to Sigismund's firmness the council stayed together. It now had to decide whether to submit to a runaway, unworthy and questionable pope and to let the schism persist or to reconstitute itself and to declare itself validly representative of the Church, even without or against doubtful popes. Would the heresy clause not justify such a procedure? Without doubt. But this was the point at which the door was opened to the radical ideas of Marsilio.

On March 23 Gerson made his famous speech to the council.[72] "The final norm, set by the Holy Spirit and transmitted by Christ, is the Church or the general council which represents the Church; every man, the pope included, must listen to her and obey. The general council is the assembly summoned by the legitimate authority from all ranks of the *hierarchy*. Every faithful has the right to be heard by it. It is the task of the council to regulate, by means of salutary discussion and decisions, whatever is necessary for the right government of the Church in faith and morals. When the Church or the general council has laid down something for the government of the Church, the pope is not above all law, not even above positive law, so that he is not at liberty to undo such decisions. Although on the other hand, the general council can in no way suspend the pope's plenitude of power which rests on the supernatural foundation made by Christ, it can nevertheless limit this power according to given rules and

[72] *Ibid.*, pp. 265ff. For what follows see my study in *Konstanz*, pp. 93ff.

laws for the edification of the Church, for the sake of which the authority of the pope as of any other man has been instituted."

"The Church or the general council has been and is able to meet in many cases without the explicit consent or order of the pope even when he has been lawfully elected and lives decently. One of these cases arises when a pope has been accused and summoned to listen to the Church according to the word of the Gospel to which he, too, is subject, and then obstinately refuses to convoke the Church; another case, when a general council has to take important decisions concerning the government of the Church, but the pope obstinately refuses to convoke it; other cases, when a general council has already decided to meet again within a certain time, or when in circumstances of genuine doubt there are several claimants to the papacy."

It is noteworthy that Gerson emphasized the hierarchical order with the pope at its head. This was not according to Marsilio's ideas. If, at the same time, he strengthened the position of the council, the reason for this lay in the prevailing situation and corresponded to the general law applied to individual cases. These statements by Gerson can and must be interpreted in a conservative sense. This makes it understandable that they met with general approval and contributed to the continuance of the council. During the session of March 26, the first one without the pope, Cardinal Zabarella proposed that the council should declare its legitimate status, should proceed in orderly fashion, not consider itself dissolved by the pope's flight, but continue "in its integrity and authority", even if the pope took measures to the contrary. It should in any case not dissolve before having finished its tasks, the ending of the schism and the reform of the Church in head and members.[73]

Meanwhile the pope tried with all his might to confuse and break up the council. There was a split in the council. The majority of the cardinals still supported John and could not imagine a council without him. The Italian section, numerically the strongest, were loyal to him. But the other three national sec-

[73] Mansi, XXVII, pp. 580ff.

tions were determined to continue the council a all costs. They summarized their position in four articles of which the first is particularly important: "The Council declares that it is lawfully assembled in the Holy Spirit, that it represents the whole militant Church as an ecumenical council and that its authority is immediately derived from God. Every Christian, the pope included, must obey the council in what concerns the faith, the ending of the schism and the reform of the Church in head and members. Whosoever obstinately refuses to accept the relevant decisions of this present or any other legitimate general council in the future, shall be punished, even if he is the pope." [74]

Negotiations took place to bring the other participants into line. It is interesting to see which points caused difficulty. The cardinals merely objected to the claim that the council reserved the reform in head and members to itself; the reform of the head was not its business, for only the pope could deal with it. The reform of the members was equally a matter for the pope. There were, however, no objections to the council's claim to be a lawful assembly and to derive its authority immediately from God. Apparently even the cardinals who were otherwise keen on safeguarding papal rights saw no difficulty in the claim that the pope owed obedience to the council. In this way the fathers came to an agreement in the fourth public session on March 30, 1415[75] and it was even hoped to persuade John.

Then John fled from Schaffhausen to Breisach on March 29, and reversed the situation once more. It was in the ensuing confusion, a mixture of despair and anger with regard to the pope, that the decree *Haec sancta* was drafted at the fifth general session of April 6, 1415. It contained again the addition "and the general reform . . . in head and members".[76]

[74] Von der Hardt, *op. cit.*, IV, p. 81.
[75] The fourth public session accepted the wording of *Haec sancta,* but the council's claim to reform the Church in head and members was omitted by Card. Zabarella. Cf. Von der Hardt, *op. cit.,* IV, p. 89; Mansi, XXVII, p. 585.
[76] The text of the decree may be found in *Conciliorum Oecumenicorum Decreta* (Freiburg, 1962), p. 385.

There is no room here to deal in a more detailed way with the circumstances of this fifth session. But we must hold on to the fact that this decree *Haec sancta* has to count as a valid decree of an ecumenical council. The question is, what is its theological significance? Can and should it be granted dogmatic validity? To deal with this difficult problem we have to look briefly at the composition of the conciliar assembly. The participants themselves are in the best situation to tell us what they had in mind.[77]

Haec sancta has been described as "the most revolutionary document in the world's history".[78] From what has been said so far it is clear that this is an exaggeration. It is quite certain that the vast majority of the council fathers had no intention of bringing about a revolution in the organization of the Church. For them the decree was an emergency measure, demanded by the need to get over the crisis in the council and to mend the split.[79] Beyond this, they did not want to limit themselves to this one case, as it presented itself in Constance, but they wanted also to take care of the future. For most of them the decree was basically a new formulation of the old rule about exceptions, which was founded on the heresy clause in canon law. According to law, therefore, a general council could consider itself "lawfully assembled in the Holy Spirit . . . in order to pursue the more easily . . . the reunion and reform of the Church of God", when the pope had deviated from the faith or had failed morally. As the papal link had fallen out in this case the council, supported only by the bishops, held its power "immediately from Christ" and the (heretical!) pope owed it obedience "in matters which concerned the faith and the elimination of the said schism"; the pope, who in reality was only a pseudo-pope, was subject to penalties if he did not obey the decisions taken by "this sacred synod and any other general council lawfully assembled".

To extend the position and task of the council beyond the emergency to a lasting control over the papacy was, frankly,

[77] See again *Konstanz*, pp. 103ff.
[78] B. Tierney, *Foundations*, p. 6, quoting J. Figgis.
[79] ". . . in order to achieve the more easily . . . reunion and reform."

difficult to reconcile with the traditional teaching. This tendency was emphasized when the council was put in charge of the *reformatio in capite et membris* generally and in principle, also in normal times. The *reformatio in capite* could provide the council at any time with an occasion to intervene with the slogan that the papacy needed reforming. The cardinals saw this danger at once and protested. The majority were also against such an extension of the council's competence with regard to the papacy. Only because of this could Cardinal Zabarella take the risk of omitting it when he read it out at the fourth session. On March 30, the decree *Haec sancta* was accepted without the addition *"ac generalem reformationem in capite e membris"*. On the part of the council fathers there was no important protest against this move of Zabarella. This proves how little influence the strict "conciliarists" had and also that, for the rest, the decree (without this addition) was understood in a conservative sense by the majority.

The change came about between March 30 and April 6. John's second flight and his deceitful behavior angered the assembly, making it lapse into a radicalism which took the shape of fierce indignation against the pope during the fifth session. Suspecting mischief, four cardinals stayed away, among them d'Ailly, but not until after having formally declared before a notary that they did not want to give their consent to any radical decrees.[80] As a matter of fact, the session was dominated by the agitators. And so, after fierce debates, the decree was finally accepted with the addition mentioned above.

Should we take it that the radical conciliarist line was now generally accepted? Did the council intend to impose "conciliarism" as a dogmatic principle by accepting this addition? For this was indeed the issue.

The cardinals certainly did not intend this; they were definitely opposed to it. The majority did not intend it either because a few days before they had taken the opposite line; clearly not realizing what the conciliarists were doing, they understood the

[80] Von der Hardt, *op. cit.*, IV, p. 97; cf. Franzen, *Konstanz*, pp. 100ff.

decree in the conservative sense. So there remained only the conciliarists with the Paris theologians at their head and led by Gerson. The question of their inner attitude, at this moment, toward the structural problem of the Church may be left open; we know Gerson's attitude. But it is important for us to know that it was the conciliarists who did not attribute infallibility in principle to the council but to the universal Church; they were therefore less interested in the decree as such than in its subsequent reception by the Church at large. Their main purpose was then to fight for the recognition and acceptance of the decrees by the Church after the council was over.

The historian can, therefore, reasonably maintain that the Council of Constance did not intend the decree *Haec sancta* to be a norm of the faith, as none of the participants meant to define an infallible dogma. The decree is not the kind of dogmatic conciliar definition which Vatican Council I describes.

We must now turn to the decree *Frequens* of the 39th session on October 9, 1417. It laid down that, in the future, general councils should be held regularly, the first after five years, the second after seven and the rest every ten years. It has been said that the purpose of this decree was to turn the organization of the Church into a constitutional monarchy and to introduce the parliamentary system. It has been supposed to be a confirmation of *Haec sancta* and a means of establishing once and for all the superiority of the council over the papacy.

These conclusions seem wrong to me. What could the periodic convocation achieve in practice? A parliament which, by law, meets only every ten years cannot really be said to lay the foundation for a parliamentary system. The decree *Frequens* did not endanger the stability of the Church's organization.

But something else happened in the debates on the reform decrees of the 39th session. The question was whether they would elect first the new pope and then proceed with and through him to the business of the reform, or whether they would first tackle the reform, thereby emphasizing the council's own right in this field, and only then choose the pope. The

latter procedure would correspond to a conciliarist interpretation of the decree *Haec sancta,* which assigned the *reformatio in
capite et membris* to the council. The reform of the Church had
always been the task of the normal ecclesiastical authority. Who
would in future exercise this normal authority, the council or
the pope? The question caused a split, and the answer was to
show whether the majority at the council thought on conciliarist
lines or not.

In the general assembly of September 9, 1417, when Sigismund and the German group insisted obstinately and threaten-
ingly that the reform should be tackled first as a concern of the
council in the sense of *Haec sancta,* they met with sharp opposition from the whole assembly.[81] Long pent-up resentment broke
through and the debates proceeded in an unusual manner. When
at last Sigismund and the Germans left the assembly under loud
protest, there were shouts of *"Recedant haeretici!"* (Heretics
outside!). They were accused of wanting to do away with the
papacy, like Huss the heretic. Only the Germans interpreted
Haec sancta in the radical conciliarist sense.

In a moderate sense, however, both *Frequens* and *Haec sancta*
were and should be understood not as in opposition to the
papacy but as subsidiary to it. The idea of the Church's co-
responsibility at the councils should be stressed. In order to
prevent an absolutist papacy, which convoked these councils
once in a century, from letting them lapse into oblivion, the
fathers laid down a minimum interval of ten years. Even more
important, the Church's right to convoke in future emergencies
was legally formulated in the following decree.[82] This action,
too, shows that the assembly was against a rigid conciliarist interpretation of *Haec sancta.* If the intention of *Haec sancta* had
been to assert the autonomy of the synod, there would have
been no need for another decree to deal with emergency measures.

---

[81] D'Ailly and Gerson also explicitly defended the rights of the papacy.
Cf. Fliche-Martin, XIV, pp. 197ff.; J. McGowan, *op. cit.,* pp. 83ff.
[82] Von der Hardt, *op. cit.,* pp. 1435ff.

For the rest *Frequens* is a disciplinary measure without dogmatic significance.

III

ECCLESIOLOGICAL SIGNIFICANCE OF THE CONSTANCE DECREES AND THEIR CONFIRMATION BY MARTIN V AND EUGENE IV

It is easy to see that these two problems are closely connected. Unless we understand what was debated and how these decrees were understood at the time, it is impossible to understand the problem of their confirmation. And on that depends our present attitude toward them.

There is no doubt that our view of the events of Constance has been strongly influenced by the later development of the conciliarist movement at the Council of Basle. Because the fathers of Basle, after their break with the pope, took up *Haec sancta* once more and used it in a radical conciliarist sense and as a dogmatic statement in their own decree *Sacrosancta* (May 16, 1439), the Council of Constance got the reputation of having defined the superiority of the council over the papacy and of having laid down a basic law for the Church's organization. Quite recently R. Bäumer still wrote: "The decrees of Constance meant a victory for conciliarism",[83] although he toned it down afterward by adding, with reference to H. Jedin: "But, as Jedin rightly emphasizes, they constituted no complete (victory) and certainly not a final one." This author saw the reason for the failure of the "conciliarist" movement of Constance in the fact that Martin V sought "to deprive these decrees of their obligatory character" and in that the papalists managed to carry on the fight for their own views which finally carried the day.

This and similar views of the events of Constance seem to me based on the false assumption that the general and most influential opinion at Constance was that of the conciliarists, and that

---

[83] R. Bäumer, "Die Stellungnahme Eugens IV, zum Konstanzer Superioritätsdekret in der Bulle *Etsi non dubitemus*," in Franzen, *Konstanz,* p. 337.

the papalist opposition could assert itself again only after the council. History shows another picture: the majority of the council was conservative and wanted no revolution in Church organization. They were mainly concerned with healing the split. For this purpose they used the means available in canon law (the heresy clause) so that they could protect the council's own authority by law against papal attacks and at the same time force these popes to submit to the council's power to restore order. So far J. Hollnsteiner has been proven correct in maintaining that *Haec sancta* must be understood as an emergency measure.[84] One should add, however, that, contrary to Hollnsteiner's opinion, it was not intended to limit its bearing to the emergency situation of 1415, but rather extend its application to similar emergencies in the future. This procedure had been prepared by medieval canon law which allowed the use of *epikeia* in an emergency on the ground of the heresy clause and had recourse for this to a legal fiction: the heretical pope was but a pseudo-pope and had to be discarded. The decree *Haec sancta* sought to lift this arrangement above the uncertainties implied in *epikeia* and to make it part of lasting emergency legislation, in other words, to give it legal force.

The majority understood and accepted the decree in this way. They felt the need to strengthen conciliar authority in face of the evil experience they had had with the three popes. The popes refused till the end to consent to the convocation of the council and then did all they could to deprive it of its legal status and so to force its dissolution: this was the true situation at the beginning of April, 1415 when *Haec sancta* was formulated. Finally, they refused to obey a council called to save the Church, on the basis of an exaggerated papalist interpretation of the primacy. This shocking condition had already lasted for forty years. It could arise again at any time. Even at this moment it had not yet been remedied. In the light of this situation the whole meaning of *Haec sancta* can be understood without difficulty.

[84] J. Hollnsteiner, in *Mitteilungen des Instituts für Oesterreichische Geschichtsforschung,* suppl. 11 (1929), p. 417; R. Bäumer, *op. cit.,* p. 339.

But even so it was still ambivalent. The conciliarists could interpret this legalization of *epikeia* in the sense of a permanent legal claim of the council against the pope. The possibility of such an interpretation was no doubt present in the document. It would need only a short leap to pass from an emergency measure to a permanent one, in order to extend the council's basic superiority over a heretical pope to a superiority over the papacy as such. The question therefore arose: who was ultimately responsible for governing the Church—a burning question when the Church's reform was debated. The words in the passage of *Haec sancta* which referred to the "general reform of the Church of God in its head and members" were interpreted by Sigismund, the Germans and a few Englishmen as declaring the council's supremacy and withholding supremacy from the pope. But they were firmly opposed by all the other participants, including the Paris theologians (d'Ailly, Gerson and others); the assembly rejected any limitation of papal power in the normal government of the Church.

The ambivalence of the decree soon led to lively discussions of its interpretation and binding force. "Since the days of the Council of Constance" this question "has remained a bone of contention between papalists and conciliarists".[85] It played a decisive part at the Council of Basle (especially after its break with the pope in 1437), at the Reformation, at the outbreak of Gallicanism, in the conflict with Febronianism and Episcopalism, and lastly at Vatican Council I. Quite recently it has stirred up renewed interest and has become actual once again in connection with the ecclesiological discussions of Vatican Council II.[86]

Recent studies try to use fully the latest research of Tierney, Ullmann and others and to advance various moderate interpretations. First among these was P. de Vooght who, dealing with

[85] R. Bäumer, *ibid.*, p. 337.
[86] H. Hürten, "Zur Ekklesiologie der Konzilien von Konstanz und Basel," in *Theologische Revue* 59 (1963), pp. 362-73; W. Beuning, in *Theologische Revue* 59 (1963), pp. 321-32; K. Smyth, "Forms of Church Government," in *Irish Theol. Quart.* 30 (1963), pp. 53-66; J. Beumer, in *Scholastik* 38 (1963), pp. 262ff.

these problems in several basic studies[87] in a personal way, met with some criticism. His thesis is that *Haec sancta did* uphold the conciliar theory and that the council formally defined it. According to him, "it was commonly accepted at Constance that in matters of faith and Church government not the pope but the council had the last word".[88] The council fathers had declared unequivocally that the council alone "was the supreme court of appeal in matters of faith in an absolute sense," not only in exceptional cases but also normally.[89] The decree *Frequens* had completed this definition of the conciliar theory and had once again confirmed that in future the Church should be governed by councils.[90] Martin V, who, according to this same author, was himself a "moderate" conciliarist, had confirmed this teaching at least silently and by implication in his bull *Inter cunctas* of February 22, 1418,[91] although in practice he shelved it again by forbidding appeals to the council. Even Eugene IV had approved the conciliarist decrees in his bull *Dudum sacrum* of December 15, 1433 "in a moment of weakness".[92]

From what I have said before it is clear that I cannot follow de Vooght. Nevertheless, I agree with him that the decrees had no binding force on the dogmatic level,[93] although I cannot accept his reasons. He thinks that, by themselves, the decrees claimed dogmatic validity but that the papal confirmation by Martin and Eugene lacked the conditions necessary for an *ex cathedra* pronouncement by Vatican Council I—the only reason why these decrees lack this validity.

[87] Cf. *supra*, n. 8; to be added: P. de Vooght, "Le conciliarisme aux conciles de Constance et de Bâle," in *Irenikon* 36 (1963), pp. 61-75; *idem*, "L'attitude des papaes Martin V et Eugène IV à l'égard du conciliarisme," *ibid.*, pp. 326-32; *idem*, "Le concile oecuménique de Constance et le conciliarisme," in *Istina* 9 (1963), pp. 57-86; *idem*, "Le Cardinal Cesarini et le Concile de Constance," in Franzen, *Konstanz*, pp. 357-80.

[88] *Idem, Das Konzil und die Konzile, op. cit.*, p. 176.

[89] *Ibid.*, p. 175.

[90] *Ibid.*, pp. 173 and 176.

[91] *Ibid.*, p. 186.

[92] *Ibid.*, p. 198.

[93] *Ibid.*, p. 209.

Hans Küng, in his fundamental study on the structures of the Church, has maintained that the decrees are still dogmatically binding. He insists, however, that the decree does not essentially define "a conciliar parliamentary system in the sense adopted by radical conciliarists," but rather "a definite kind of superiority of the council in the sense of an at least moderately 'conciliar theory'." [94] This superiority was fitted to the emergency of those days, but also granted the council "a kind of controlling appellate function above the pope whose lapse into heresy, schism, etc. remained a basic possibility"; and the council would have this function in similar emergencies. However much I agree with Küng's interpretation of the contents of the decree, I disagree with him on the point of a dogmatic binding force, because the facts of history contradict it.

Hubert Jedin[95] has also stressed the emergency character of the decrees of Constance. According to him *Haec sancta* in no sense presupposes Marsilio's dogmatically untenable democratic notion of the Church, nor the purely spiritual conception of Wycliffe or Huss, nor the extreme papalist notion which made the pope a kind of embodiment of the universal Church. That is why the council's claim truly to represent the Church as an ecumenical council cannot be contested. The difficulties arise from the council's claim that its authority is immediately derived from Christ and that it must be obeyed by everyone, the pope included, in matters of faith, Church unity and reform. This contains the essence of the conciliar theory: the council claims to be above the pope.

Jedin, however, has clearly demonstrated that *Haec sancta* represented "a solution at a moment of extreme danger" and that it "was not a general statement of the faith, suspended, so to speak, in midair, but rather . . . an emergency measure for a

---

[94] H. Küng, *Strukturen der Kirche*, 2nd ed. (Freiburg, 1963), pp. 259 and 269; see also *idem, Structures of the Church* (New York: Nelson, 1963).

[95] H. Jedin, *Bischöfliches Konzil oder Kirchenparlament. Ein Beitrag zur Ekklesiologie der Konzilien von Konstanz und Basel* (Basle-Stuttgart, 1963.

clearly defined exceptional case".[96] Like every conciliar decision, this one, too, must be interpreted in the light of its circumstances. The interpretation of the decree as an emergency measure seems to be contradicted by its demand, backed by sanctions, that the pope should obey the decisions, not only of this council, but "of any other general council lawfully assembled". When Küng, de Vooght and others draw the conclusion that these words establish the claim of the decree to absolute validity, they over-look the fact that a sanction cannot extend beyond the law;[97] when therefore the law is merely concerned with emergency situations, now and in the future, then the sanction, too, can only affect those popes who would again endanger the Church through heresy, schism, etc., which would need "another law-fully summoned general council" to deal with them.

I agree with Jedin's verdict, as is clear from the historical situation as I have tried to analyze it above. But I would like to stress still more the connection of *Haec sancta* with the medieval tradition of canon law: *Haec sancta* is the legalization of the Church's right to deal with emergencies, which medieval law developed from the heresy clause and which was now accepted by the Church as law. The majority of the council fathers was conservative-minded. The contrary view of a predominantly conciliarist majority is a myth. The conciliarists were a minority, and not even a united minority. Moreover, the dividing line be-tween the ideas of the real conservatives, in favor of reform but opposed to innovation, and the moderate conciliarists who clung to the basic hierarchical structure of the Church was very thin and fluid. The decree itself was open to various interpretations. For example, "conciliarists" like d'Ailly and Gerson refused to deprive the pope of the power to reform and govern the Church in normal times and to hand it over to the council; they inter-preted this passage of the decree in a conservative and not in a conciliarist sense. Yet, having learned their lesson from past experiences, they opposed extreme papalism in any form. And

---

[96] *Ibid.*, p. 12.
[97] *Ibid.*, pp. 31ff.

so Gerson protested fiercely against Pope Martin's prohibition of appeals to the council on May 10, 1418, because he was afraid of a return of papal absolutism.[98]

To conclude: in *Haec sancta* the Council of Constance neither proclaimed nor intended to proclaim an irrevocable dogmatic definition. It merely incorporated an existing positive law in general law and so turned it from an obscure, controversial canonical regulation into a proper law which could deal with any such cases in the future on a legal basis. Under the influence of the peculiar historical circumstances certain formulas (about the general reform etc.) came in with it. The formulas originating in the conciliarist sector, though open to a conciliarist interpretation, were taken by the majority in the conservative sense. Only at the Council of Basle were the conciliarist elements of *Haec sancta* turned into a dogmatic pronouncement in the decree *Sacrosancta*.

The question whether Martin V and Eugene IV accepted the decrees of the Council of Constance has been hotly debated from the beginning and has recently again become the subject of lively discussion. While P. de Vooght insisted that both Martin and Eugene formally approved these decrees,[99] H. Küng has come to the conclusion that the relevant statements of Martin V did not constitute "a formal approval in the technical sense" but expressed Martin's overall agreement.[100] On the other hand, in a careful analysis of the texts R. Bäumer[101] reached an opposite conclusion: by the sharp tone of his prohibition of appeals to

---

[98] Gerson, "Tractatus quomodo et an," in *Gersonis Opera* Vol. 2 (ed. L. E. du Pin, Antwerp, 1706), pp. 303-8, written in May 1418 at Constance. Cf. R. Bäumer, "Das Verbot der Konzilsappellation Martins V. in Konstanz," in Franzen, *Konstanz*, pp. 187-213, esp. 200ff. Gerson was opposed to the prohibition of appeal in principle, not to a limited prohibition. According to Bäumer, the pope meant this prohibition as a matter of principle (Bäumer also indicates that the date of May 10, 1418 is wrong).

[99] Most recently in Franzen, *Konstanz*, p. 357: "I believe I have shown in several previous studies that Martin V and Eugene IV approved the decrees from the third to the fifth sessions of the Council of Constance."

[100] H. Küng, *op. cit.*, pp. 250 and 253.

[101] R. Bäumer, *loc. cit.*, p. 187; *idem*, "Die Stellungnahme Eugens IV," *ibid.*, p. 339.

the council Martin took the wind out of the sails of *Haec sancta* and this attitude of rejection was consistently maintained by Eugene. Although he had to approve the Council of Basle, he "never confirmed the decree on the superiority of the council explicitly and by name, not even in the bull *Dudum sacrum* of December 15, 1433, but rather rejected it in his bull *Etsi non dubitemus* of April 20, 1441".[102] Jedin, too, thinks there can be no doubt that "in spite of the duress they were under—since their own legitimacy depended on the election at Constance—Martin V and Eugene IV never declared themselves in agreement with the general and absolute validity of the decree *Haec sancta,* and never formally confirmed it".[103]

In fact, the initial hesitation of the two popes can be adequately explained by the ambivalence of the decree. They had no objection to a conservative interpretation. In the long run they had to realize that extreme conciliarists tried to impose upon it a radical interpretation; consequently, they opposed it. The break of the Basle conciliarists with the pope clarified the situation in 1437. The conciliarists failed to win acceptance of the Constance decrees. Neither the popes, nor the Christian people at large[104] accepted conciliarism, and since by then the conservative interpretation had been forgotten, the decrees were rejected by the Church along with the rejection of conciliarism. The Council of Constance itself became, as we know now, most unjustly suspect.

[102] *Ibid.,* pp. 339ff.
[103] H. Jedin, *op. cit.,* p. 17.
[104] Instances of this in German are given by H. Hürten, *op. cit.,* pp. 369ff. How the attitude toward the decrees of Constance changed in individual cases has been shown by P. de Vooght with regard to Cardinal Cesarini (cf. Franzen, *Konstanz,* pp. 357-80) and by H. Hürten with regard to Nicholas of Cusa (*ibid.,* pp. 381-96).

Giuseppe Alberigo/*Bologna, Italy*

The Council of Trent

New Views on the Occasion
of Its Fourth Centenary

I

SIGNIFICANCE OF TRIDENTINE HISTORIOGRAPHY

1. *Evolution of Tridentine Historiography*

The Council of Trent has experienced a singular fate and has occupied an unaccustomed place—even for a great ecumenical council—in the life of the Church. This singularity has also been manifested by the formation of its own valid historiographical tradition, developed over the centuries.[1] Manifold reasons for this fact—unique in conciliar history—can be found initially in the exceptional importance to the Church of the Tridentine decisions. Moreover, convened at the beginning of modern times, the council was contemporaneous with the birth of historical science in the modern sense and with the decisive turn that characterized the new orientation of ecclesiastical historiography caused by Protestant-Catholic polemics.

Consequently, beginning with the diaries kept by some of the council participants up to the refined historical studies of the last few years, Trent has constituted a memorable chapter of ecclesiastical historiography. Such a chapter now spans four cen-

[1] Cf. the profound study of H. Jedin, *Das Konzil von Trient. Ein Ueberblick über die Erforschung seiner Geschichte* (Rome, 1948).

turies and has often faithfully mirrored the evolution of the general orientations of the Church. Throughout this development it is fairly easy to discover how much the manner of conceiving and writing the history of the Council of Trent was affected by the fact that it was not a completely historicized event concluded long ago, but rather an active and operative factor, absolutely decisive in many aspects of the Church's life. Rarely could the historian's work completely escape the actual implications which the object of his study continued to have.

Such a basic conditioning of Tridentine historiography must be kept in mind as a factor (even if only implicit), constantly figuring in its development as regards the choice of themes, the type of historical reconstruction and finally the very elaboration of research methods.

This consideration, in a certain sense preliminary and prejudicial, must not be mistaken for an insuperable obstacle to true historical research which might substantially undermine the scientific value of Tridentine studies. It refers rather to the "climate" in which Tridentine historiography has developed. The Tridentine atmosphere is obviously different from the more rarefied and detached climate which gave birth to the historiography of past councils or of the majority of historical events in the Church, now definitively and irreversibly concluded as facts (having a beginning and an end) or as the consequences of these facts, which become directed, absorbed and overshadowed by succeeding events.

2. The Controversialist Phase

A reliable, historical study on the Council of Trent not only is possible but has been impressively achieved by the development and progress of Tridentine historiography. This development has taken place in several fundamental stages. Until the end of the 19th century, studies concerning the council were hampered by the serious objective limitation of partial, fragmentary and often indirect historical documentation. As long as the imposing Tridentine source in the secret Vatican archives remained inaccessible, no historian—despite every effort at documentation and despite any fortunate archival *trouvaille*—possessed a complete and certain knowledge of the sources. Under these conditions, the validity and rigor of the studies gradually appearing was radically impaired and an atmosphere of strong polemical tension between Catholics and Protestants began to emerge. The result was a literature very profuse but of predominantly controversial inspiration, whose extremes were the works of the Venetian Servite Paolo Sarpi and the Jesuit Pallavicino Sforza. Although using primary sources with reference to Trent, they nonetheless imposed on the council the historical reconstruction dictated by their convictions—antipathetic for Sarpi and apologetic for Sforza.

Later, the lack of a *corpus* of truly complete and exhaustive sources delayed the end of the long controversialist phase of Tridentine historiography when every scholar could choose too freely—and hence often arbitrarily—which sources to accredit and use. Only the courageous and liberating decisions of Leo XIII, who threw open to scholars all the official documentation jealously preserved in the Vatican archives, inaugurated a new phase. The fruitful zeal and scientific precision of the scholars of the Görres-Gesellschaft, later joined by scholars of other countries, was able to prepare, in a manner worthy of admiration and gratitude, an edition of the Tridentine sources systematized according to four documentary series: Diaries, Acts, Correspondence and Tracts.[2]

Between 1901 and 1938 eleven volumes *in quarto* were published, and another two have been added in recent years. Scholars then had the use of almost the entire documentation, both official and private, comprising principally the diaries of the Council Secretary, the official records of the sessions, the correspondence between the papal legates at Trent and Rome and the tracts com-

---

[2] *Concilium Tridentinum. Diariorum, Actorum, Epistolarum, Tractatuum, Nova Collectio*, ed. Societas Görresiana, 14 Vols. (Freiburg im Breisgau, 1901-61). Since 1964 out-of-print volumes are in the process of being anastatically reprinted.

posed on occasion of the council. A decisive forward step had
been taken. There now existed a documentary basis whose rigor
and reliability were unanimously and unreservedly acknowledged. Not only did this make possible studies previously completely excluded (e.g., on the formation of the individual decrees), but the way was now open toward a global historical
reconstruction of the entire development of the council which
would surpass the works of Sarpi and Pallavicino in rigorously
scientific inspiration and in a complete and easily controlled
documentary basis.

3. The Critical Phase

The same German scholarship, which in dedicating itself so
austerely to historical studies had always exhibited a particularly
alert awareness of the religious division of the 16th century, now
produced the man capable of bringing to fruition the new course
of Tridentine historiography. With authentic historical sense
Hubert Jedin put to good use the imposing works already published during the first four decades of the century. Indeed, it is
reasonable to suppose that had it not been for the intervention
of a chaotic war, Jedin would almost certainly have succeeded
in making the publication of his *History of the Council of Trent*
coincide with the celebration of the fourth centenary of the Council in 1945.[3] In the meantime the complete accessibility of
sources spurred a vast revival of studies concerning the external
history of Trent, the development of individual debates on various arguments for dogma and reform, and the content of the
decrees and their influence on the subsequent life of the Church.[4]

---

[3] In fact, the first volume appeared in 1949 almost contemporaneously
at Freiburg im Breisgau in the original German and at Brescia in Italian
translation; in subsequent years translations into the other principal languages followed (English: Vol. 1 and Vol. 2 published by Herder and
Herder, New York; Vol. 3 in prep.). In 1957 the second volume was issued, containing the exposition of the events of the council up to its
transferal to Bologna in March 1547. Two other volumes are anticipated.
[4] Jedin published in 1951 an ample review of the studies that had appeared with relation to the first phase of the centenary celebrations: "Das
vierhundertjährige Jubiläum der Eröffnung des Konzils von Trient und

Another positive contribution was made by the historical turn taken in the last few decades by studies in theology and canon law. Although they have often dwelt on a limited point, isolating it excessively from its general context, they provided important sources and offered a basis for historical reflection.

Tridentine historiography has thus emerged from a controversialist phase and, after finally gaining a documentary basis, has assumed a scientific dignity in the last few decades. The image of the great council of the 16th century has taken on precise and definite outlines, the reward of a rigorous analysis of the sources. Centuries-old, *a priori* polemics were gently erased by the clear light of factual truth. Jedin's work is especially decisive in this respect. His *History* escapes from the legacy of defamation and apologia to reach the plateau of what actually occurred. Trent thus casts aside superfluous accretions which adversaries and defenders alike had combined to heap on it, falsely making it either a "legend" of decadence, or of ecclesial renewal and inexhaustible fecundity. Jedin placed Trent in its true context: (a) by a better understanding of the political and social factors that influenced it; (b) by a better understanding of the influence exerted by the general religious situation of Christianity (constrained to emerge almost without warning and all at once from the medieval equilibrium that had been again laboriously restored after the Western Schism); and (c) by a better understanding of the incidence of various orientations present in Christianity itself. The Council of Trent was indeed a fact of exceptional proportions and significance, yet always in a definite historical context. It was, therefore, understandable only if studied without losing sight of the conditioning factors of such a context.

In like manner, the internal history of developments during the sessions (such as the debates on doctrine and reform) is now

---

seiner wissenschaftlicher Ertrag," in *Das Weltkonzil von Trient* Vol. 1 (Freiburg im Breisgau: G. Schreiber, 1951), pp. 11-31; see also the "Bulletin d'histoire des doctrines chrétiennes" of the *Revue de sciences philosophiques et theologiques* published by A. Duval under the title *Autour du centenaire du Concile de Trente* 31 (1947), pp. 241-71 and 36 (1952), pp. 538-44.

reconstructed on the results of a multiple documentation, whether official or private. By means of this documentation, the various phases and acts of the council acquire their proper and distinguishing characteristics. The eighteen years from 1545 to 1563 are animated by an incessant dynamism in the midst of which even the most relevant acts—such as the dogmatic Decree on Justification of 1546 or the disciplinary decrees of 1563—can be seen and appraised as related to a certain time, to specific problems and to a definite group of men. This fundamental process of historicization has established the decisive premises for an articulate and realistic evaluation of the conciliar decisions. The method discerns their value as well as their limitations; in arriving at their true significance, it cuts away the incrustations which the work of interpretation and subsequent implementation gradually added, at times rendering the decisions themselves irreconcilable.

4. The Real Council and Its Implementation

Although the *History* of Jedin and other enlightening studies are still incomplete,[5] the Council of Trent can today be understood much more fully than in the past. It appears as an ecclesiastical assembly made up of bishops coming almost exclusively from countries faithful to Rome. Papal legates, some of whom were of great historical stature, presided; the council was summoned to construct a dam capable of confronting and repelling the destructive wave of the Lutheran Reformation that had erupted in Germany and was flooding the entire Church. In addition to the work of safeguarding traditional doctrine, the council grappled with the problem of moral reform; such a reform was the constant but frustrated hope of a century, and the popes themselves saw that it could no longer be postponed.

It is well known that the council, subjected to opposing pres-

[5] On the occasion of the fourth centenary of the conclusion of the council, he published a summary sketch of the last period which ends with a global evaluation. It expresses judgments often analogous to those found in these pages: *Der Abschluss des Trienter Konzils 1562-1563. Ein Rückblick nach vier Jahrhunderten* (Münster, 1964).

sures from various sources, resolved to attack in parallel fashion both the dogmatic problems and those concerning reform. Their constant guide was the principle of providing for various necessities from time to time, without ever pretending to develop an integrated and complete plan which would scarcely have been understood by those lacking—as was true of the overwhelming majority of the fathers—a clear concept of the Church.[6] The starting point was the fact that the Protestant Reformation had dealt a massive blow to the ecclesiological order developed during the Middle Ages. Doctrinal restoration and an indispensable and energetic reform of customs were necessary, yet they avoided touching upon the problems concerning the structure of the Church. In this perspective, the council systematically limited itself to individual acts of reform or doctrinal explanation. Thus they filled a leak in the existing system which did not quite demand a complete and exhaustive doctrine. Such an orientation, substantially unsystematic and fragmentary, was subsequently confirmed by the external events of the council which, lasting eighteen years with very lengthy adjournments, witnessed the succession of five popes and acquired a total of thirteen different papal legates.

Between the opening and definitive closing of the council, few indeed were the bishops who had not been reassigned, so profoundly altered was the whole political, social and religious face of Europe and of the entire world. Especially altered were the prospects of the great religious question tearing Europe apart: although the council had met in the hope of reducing heresy and reuniting the dissident "Protestants", such hopes were already growing dim at the end of the council. Protestantism then constituted a world in itself which showed no hopeful sign of reuniting with Rome in the near future, particularly on the basis of Tridentine decrees. When the work of implementing the conciliar decisions got underway at the end of the pontificate of Pius IV, it became all too apparent that the situation posed a much more

[6] Cf. G. Alberigo, "L'ecclesiologia del Concilio di Trento," in *Rivista di Storia della Chiesa in Italia* 17 (1964), pp. 227-42.

serious task than the already difficult one of stopping the leaks in the medieval ecclesial system. In fact, the system itself no longer existed: the religious crisis, the renascence, geographic discoveries and the collapse of the imperial legend of Charles V had swept it away. A vigorous restoration of the medieval equilibrium no longer sufficed for the renewal of the Church; now there was need of a capacity to evolve a new system synthesizing Christian values and the altered historical situation. Thus emerged the basic alternative that influenced the work of implementing the council and, on a wider scale, the life of the Church in the four succeeding centuries. Confronted with the disproportion between the vast work of the council and the immense complexity of new problems to be solved by the Church, Rome found itself forced to make a decisive choice.

Fidelity to the council was for everyone beyond question. The renewal of the Church then, could have been sought through an implementation of Trent that would have filled the gaps. The true spirit of the council was to seek out anew the implicit vision of the Church shared and anticipated by many fathers who nevertheless lacked the power to delineate it in systematic fashion and with necessary clarity.[7] Charles Borromeo, for one, entertained such a vision.

Instead, the "Roman" implementation of the Council of Trent began in the other direction. The *corpus* of the conciliar decisions was presented as exhaustive and definitive; it was to constitute an inexhaustible code of prescriptions for every necessity, gradually elevated to decisive canons to which reference had to be made for all the needs of the Christian life. In this way, although the authority of the council was intransigently determined, isolating it ever more from the preceding productive tradition, there was

---

[7] Revealing in this respect is the study of H. Jedin, "Das Bischofsideal der Katholischen Reformation," in *Sacramentum Ordinis* (Breslau, 1942), pp. 200-57, amplified in the French edition of P. Broutin, *L'Evêque dans la tradition pastorale du XVIe siècle* (Brussels, 1953); H. Jedin, "Das Tridentinische Bischofsideal. Ein Literaturbericht," in *Trierer Theologische Zeitschrift* 69 (1960), pp. 237-46; and I. Tellechea Idigoras, *El Obispo ideal en el siglo de la Reforma* (Rome, 1963).

nevertheless a definite movement toward an ever wider and freer interpretation of its dogmatic and disciplinary decisions. They were interpreted according to principles and attitudes often different from, and at times even opposed to, those from which the council had taken its inspiration.

The substantial progress of Tridentine historiography enables us today to place these problems within their proper framework. It is increasingly clear that conciliar and post-conciliar events, although contiguous and complementary elements, must not be interchanged as has often happened both in the historiographical sphere and on the more delicate plane of ecclesial consciousness. The implementation of Trent did not entail merely the task of introducing the decrees to the entire Church in communion with Rome; it was itself no less a creative work and as such necessitated a whole series of choices whose relation to the spirit of the council was not always, despite repeated protestations of loyalty, either docile or clear.

5. Discussions Concerning Method and Basic Uncertainties

These are in summary fashion the conclusions of the most recent historiographic studies. Studies on Trent appear solidly anchored to a rigorously scientific foundation. In fact, this common platform has opened the way for profitable discussions concerning method, discussions intended ultimately to refine and deepen the understanding of the sources. Some scholars have raised the question of a greater sensitivity to the doctrinal dimension of the council, criticizing the *History* of Jedin for giving excessive emphasis to the external events of the council, especially those that were politico-ecclesiastical.[8] In reality, the doctrinal and spiritual history of the council has unquestionably received insufficient development up to the present time; the deepening of its dimensions depends in large measure upon the

[8] The criticisms were raised by J. Lortz, "Um das Konzil von Trient," in *Theologische Revue* 47 (1951), cols. 157-70 and discussed by Jedin, "Zur Aufgabe des Kirchengeschichtsschreibers," in *Trierer Theologische Zeitschrift* 61 (1952), pp. 65-78 and anew by Lortz, "Nochmals: zur Aufgabe des Kirchengeschichtsschreibers," *ibid.*, pp. 317-27.

progress made by the studies concerning the history of the theology and spirituality of the 16th century.

On the methodological plane, the French scholar A. Dupront has requested greater consideration for the sociological aspect.[9] The prospects for such study are decidedly opportune, though they must avoid an exclusive emphasis on sociological data, which are necessarily deficient particularly when concerned with phenomena of religious history.[10] It may perhaps be more profitable to turn the attention of Tridentine studies to the relationship of the council with the contemporary situation of the Church. In setting the council in its contemporary context, studies of this sort would reveal how this relationship influenced the orientations of the council through the bishops and theologians who embodied its meaning.[11]

The very fact that studies on Trent pose such problems is unequivocal testimony to their progress and maturity. But alongside this great harvest of positive results Tridentine historiography also presents a few obscurities. These include first of all the aspects of conciliar history that are still insufficiently explored—a limited knowledge which weighs negatively on the whole picture. This must be said of the biographical studies on the more important figures of the council, still in large part lacking though we have seen what great explicatory value vigorous biographies can have.[12] Unfortunately, however, figures like Cervini, Pole,

[9] A. Dupront, "Du Concile de Trente: réflexions autour d'un IV centenaire," in *Revue historique* 75 (1951), pp. 262-80; "Le Concile de Trente," in *Le concile et les conciles. Contribution à l'histoire de la vie conciliaire de l'Eglise* (Paris-Chevetogne, 1960), pp. 195-243; and again in the conclusions of the festive historical gathering on the fourth centenary: *Il Concilio di Trento e la Riforma Tridentina* (Trent, 1965), pp. 557-71.

[10] I have developed my reservations in "Note di storia e teologia conciliare," in *Ephemerides Theologicae Lovanienses* 40 (1964), pp. 93-7.

[11] I have given a sample of this type of research in my book: *I vescovi italiani al concilio di Trento (1545-1547)* (Florence, 1959).

[12] I recall the exemplars, each in its own sphere, of H. Jedin, *Girolamo Senprando. Sein Leben und Denken im Geisteskampf des 16 Jhr.* (Würzburg, 1937); H. Evennett, *The Cardinal of Lorraine and the Council of Trent* (Cambridge, 1930), and finally P. Prodi, *Il Cardinale Gabriele Paleotti* (Rome, 1959-1965).

Guerrero, Morone, Charles Borromeo—to mention the most important—are still known only partially and imperfectly. Their lives and actions are not stripped of the pious hagiographic lore of succeeding centuries. I have already touched upon the still too modest knowledge of the theological currents of that time and of the external and specifically conceptual proceedings of the doctrinal debates.[13]

Above all, however, one must take note of a certain ennui that has recently appeared in Tridentine studies in the last few years of the centenary celebrations. The publication of sources is lagging, in spite of the fact that the *Görres-Gesellschaft* collection is yet to be completed.[14] Among the dozens of reviews that deal with religious sciences, only a few—and all in Spanish—have celebrated the conclusion of the same centenary festivities[15] begun in 1945 with widespread and fervent study, despite the great difficulty of those precarious times.[16] Nor does it appear

[13] Cf. also G. Alberigo, "Le potesta episcopali nei dibattiti tridentini," in *Il Concilio di Trento e la Riforma Tridentina* (Trent, 1965), pp. 3-5 (provisional pagination).

[14] Besides volumes VI and VII of the *Görresiana* series only sporadic and fragmentary editions have appeared concerning the individual votes cast in the council and only in the last few months *l'Archivio Storico Italiano* 122 (1964), pp. 1-453 has published a conspicuous fund of Florentine dispatches relative to the 3rd period of the council: *Il carteggio degli ambasciatori e degli informatori medicei da Trento nella terza fase del Concilio*, while the State Archives of Rome brought to light a few of the original books of the council expenses: *Aspetti della Riforma cattolica e del Concilio de Trento. Documentary proofs. Catalogo a cuva di E. Aleandri Barletta* (Rome, 1964), pp. 95-136. Now in preparation is the publication of the Guidi diary, the last of this type of unpublished sources. A chronology of the fund indicated by H. Evennett "The Manuscripts of the Vargas-Granvelle Correspondence, 1551-2," in *Journal of Ecclesiastical History* 11 (1960), pp. 219-24 has been published by C. Gutierrez, "Nueva documentacion tridentina," in *Archivum Historiae Pontificiae* 1 (1963), pp. 179-240, adding the publication of the original of a tract on the councils by F. de Vargas, *ibid.* 2 (1964), pp. 210-50.

[15] The reviews are: *Hispania Sacra* 16 (1963), pp. 1-248 and *Estudios Eclesiasticos* 39 (1964), pp. 5-141, 147-73, 319-60 and 459-82. Ample bibliographical indications on the studies issued in the last few years are in *Archivum Historiae Pontificiae* 1 (1963), pp. 574-78 and 2 (1964), pp. 461-65.

[16] See the numerous notes published by the review *Il Concilio di Trento. Rivista Commemorativa del IV centenario*, 1942-1947 and the already cited review of Jedin. Cf. note 1.

that the recurrence of the centenary marking the beginning of the council's implementation will be any more fortunate.[17]

I believe that the basic causes of this diminution of interest are to be found directly in the present status of the Council of Trent not only in ecclesiastical history but more generally in the life of the Church.

II

THE COUNCIL OF TRENT IN THE NEW ECCLESIAL SITUATION

1. *The Predominant Function of Trent*

Up to this point, we have endeavored to discuss briefly the historiographical balancesheet with respect to Trent; now we must extend the study to a wider plane, seeking to discover the role played by Trent in the life of the Church and the Church's awareness of this role. At this level recent years have verified new findings worthy of greater consideration. One must remember that the council has exercised a far greater role in the Church than can be indicated by Tridentine studies. Indeed, rather than remaining the object of historical knowledge after the conclusion of its labors, it has experienced a long and very luxuriant period as an active and dynamic factor in the life of the Catholic Church throughout the West. For centuries after its closing we witnessed the growth rather than decline of Trent's proper prestige and authority. It was forced by circumstances to exercise a regulatory function on the entire life of the Church.

Beginning with the end of the 16th century, the popes instructed the Church to see in the council the ultimate rule of faith and discipline, naturally not in the sense that the norms established previously were superseded, but that they were in-

[17] The Congregation of Seminaries and Universities has published *Seminaria Ecclesiae Catholicae* (Rome, 1963) dedicated in great part to the listing of institutions of clerical formation. The Congregation of the Council in its turn has published a miscellany of *Studi e ricerche* (Rome, 1964) in which, however, the properly Tridentine problems have found only a very faint echo.

corporated, clarified and implemented by Trent. Hence, it was sufficient and in fact preferable to know the norms through the filtering process exercised by Trent. A list of the numerous editions of the decisions of Trent up to the eve of the Code of Canon Law (1917) will readily confirm the predominance enjoyed by the *corpus* of Tridentine decrees. Progressively excluded from ecclesiastical usage were all preceding sources, including the *Decretum Gratiani* which during the Middle Ages had largely helped to preserve some contact—even though partial and fragmentary—with Christian antiquity. Hence, it gradually became legitimate, and eventually obligatory, to refer to Trent for the solution of all problems, both doctrinal and institutional.[18] In this way the post-Tridentine Church gained a compactness which during the acute phase of the Protestant separation none would have dared believe possible; indeed, it is well known that this "Tridentine-ism" succeeded in penetrating to a significant degree into certain areas of the reformed world.

Concluded as event, the council became history; but instead of undergoing a process of decantation through the assimilation of its decisions into the Church's tradition, Trent has been elevated to the status of that very tradition after forming and integrating it into the life of the Church.

The new ecclesial system necessitated by the deterioration of the medieval equilibrium and the new exigencies of mankind was outlined in the *corpus* of the Tridentine decisions. These came to be accepted as an authoritative guide to the extent that the constitutive elements of the new system were judged positive or negative on the basis of their conformity to these decisions. This

---

[18] Occasionally in the last few years a few theologians have appeared to indulge an attitude of this type, seeking in the Tridentine decisions a solution to problems posed by modern theological research. Such for example has been the case with the relation between Scripture and Tradition, concerning which some have hoped to find a valid answer in the Tridentine debates. It has not always been kept in mind that, contrary to appearances, the context and mode of expressing similar problems is in reality much different between the 16th century and today. It is one thing to study the historical development of a question but quite another to wish to derive its solution from the past.

fact necessarily conferred on Trent a most singular prestige, which naturally redounded on historical studies. Indeed, until a few years ago, a better knowledge of its historical events did not constitute mere progress in the knowledge of the past and of Christian tradition, but contributed to a more profund knowledge of the leading ideas of the present ecclesial situation.

In this respect, the trend taken by Tridentine studies in the last few years is symptomatic. It attests that the world of scholarship has discovered—perhaps still in uncertain, confused and unconscious fashion—a substantial modification in the ecclesial status of the council. The years since 1959—to choose a commonly accepted date—have seen a profound and substantial rectification of the Catholic Church's line of historical development. This has resulted in a true and unique curve whose significance is still difficult to evaluate but which is certainly of unusual dimensions.

Some have spoken of the end of the Age of Constantine and others of the end of the Counter-Reformation, testifying to the widespread awareness of a profound modification in the ecclesiastical order which is in progress both on the conceptual as well as on the psychological and practical level. This phenomenon, whose decisive influence on the history of the Church in future centuries can be gauged even from the present, clashes with the former position of Trent in the economy of the Church, ending its predominance definitively and irreversibly. It is obviously not a question of emphasizing that a new ecumenical council overshadows the preceding; nothing similar to what is happening was noted on the occasion of Vatican Council I. Today we are in the presence of much more than a new page in conciliar history. Rather the whole system based on Trent is declining, a system that had formed slowly after the 12th century and had ruled the Western Church till a few years ago.

2. The Decline of the System Consolidated around Trent

It may be opportune to venture a closer analysis of this decline. The essential element of the Tridentine epoch's decline appears ever more clearly evident in its very own and distinctive elements, *i.e.*, those constituting its supporting structure. This signifies neither the denial of an epoch of the Church—although it would be unpardonable myopia not to recognize its decline— nor that a new and different system has already replaced the preceding one. On the contrary, these historical phenomena are inevitably complex and hence do not proceed in a unique line of progression. Indeed, they can undergo even provisional or partially inverse tendencies; while not overturning the basic system they can prolong its phases or obscure its clear general plan. To discern amidst a welter of contrasting and even contradictory facts the basic orientation that explains them can be, especially in time of transition, the highest task of a society's consciousness.

The Tridentine system, understood in the above-mentioned sense, comprised not only the nucleus of conciliar decisions, but also the ideas, the concepts, the habits, the institutional facts and the organizational practice that had been incorporated very early —between 1504 and the first decades of the 17th century—into the decisions themselves. In this we can discover, as already mentioned, a certain number of constitutive elements: first of all, a static and defensive ecclesiology based on the "societal" dimension of the Church, often at the expense of the more interior element touching upon "mystery". Under the circumstances, the exigencies of canonical structure and the defense of the traditional faith by means of controversy and repression gradually became the rule.

For its part, dogma concentrated especially on a predominantly analytic sacramental theology—and on its eventual casuistic degenerations—which refined the notion of transcendence as the essential intervention of Christ in the sacraments. This notion, clear and vigorous in the Tridentine Decree on Justification, became dimmed when an even more ample place was reserved for the human elements competing with the sacraments in the production of the effects assigned them. Characteristic examples of this are baptism and holy orders where there is required, together with their administration, other extra-sacramental elements in order to produce membership in the Church or the transmission of ministerial power respectively.

Another element destined to play a decisive role was the uncertainty of the place of Sacred Scripture in Christian life. The conciliar decree of the 4th session (1546) left open all possibilities, but the practice begun immediately afterward and the mental habit that is consolidated gravitated toward an ever more restricted and less faithful use of the Scriptures, especially the Old Testament. From such an orientation both liturgy and preaching received their formation. The liturgy, unsupported by a dynamic use of the Christian mystery and deprived of sufficient biblical sustenance, concentrated more and more on the eucharist, effectuating an imposing and beneficent spiritual period. However, partial attention, distracted from the sacrificial and communal value of the mass, dislodged eucharistic piety from its natural setting and endowed it with an individualistic bent. Preaching, for its part, suffered heavily under the influx of the literary baroque, or else took refuge in a catechetical form responding to a widespread need for religious instruction; such notional arrangements, however, were not likely to bring profound results. The general piety, unable to follow the singular mystical flights of a few elect individuals, nourished itself especially on the cult of the Blessed Virgin and the saints, accentuating the individualistic wave already manifested by Protestantism. The life of the parish as a spiritual community was dealt a staggering blow at the hands of the new orientation. Moreover, the particularistic significance reflected more and more by the churches and chapels of the mendicant orders and the new religious congregations augmented the damage. The same religious confraternities that for centuries had contributed toward the vitality of parish life by guaranteeing the supply of qualified groups were in this new context exercising a dispersive thrust.

Passing from doctrinal and spiritual factors to other aspects of the same system, we readily perceive that Church unity, the basic problem of the first half of the 16th century, had been radically shunted aside. What had been strengthened—to be sure, with pain and regret—was an acceptance both institutional and spiritual of the division of Christianity. Under these circumstances, the ecclesial mark of *unitas* was inoperative to such an extent that the very attempts for union remained nothing more than episodes, powerless not only to reconstruct unity but even to modify the interior habit of polemic and division. Unity thus became a quality to be defended jealously rather than a gift to be merited and shared.

From another point of view, the structure of the Church undoubtedly emerges strengthened thanks, above all, to a marked preponderance of the hierarchical over the communal aspect. Emphasis is placed on a vertical conception of the organization of the Church which sketches the separation between faithful and hierarchy, conceiving the latter as a "ladder" and relegating the intermediate functions ever more to the background. This results in a weakening of the minor orders with respect to the priesthood and of the episcopacy with respect to the papacy.

On the other hand, the guidance of the Church was assumed in an increasingly exclusive and direct fashion by the bishop of Rome through a series of structural reforms effectuated or brought to completion in the decades immediately following the close of the council. To that period belong the creation of the Roman congregations and the corresponding liquidation of the collegiate office of the cardinalate, the perfecting of the system of nuncios who connect the duties of diplomatic representation with those of control over the various episcopates, the widescale use of apostolic visitors and finally the attribution to religious orders of functions no longer "special" but concerned with the supporting structure of the Church. Consequently, the episcopal function became ever more circumscribed by the limits of the individual Churches and by the execution of decisions taken in other sees. This set the obligation of reform, opportunely sanctioned by the council, on the road to a voluntaristic activism sustained by canonical norms. Despite its energy, such reform exposed itself to the risk of deviating from reflection and nourishment based on Scripture and the most ancient and certain tradition. As a result, the ideal of reform took the shape of a search for good ecclesiastical order.

A last decisive element of the Tridentine system was the relationship of the Church to the world, which first resisted and eventually seceded, threatening the Church with the reduction of her boundaries to the strictly clerical sphere. Not even the missionary impetus, rich in energy and capable of frequent heroism, succeeded in substantially expanding the "European" horizon of the Church of these centuries. Attempts to widen such perspectives were regarded as a threat to the *status quo:* it suffices to recall the controversies over the Chinese rites or over the Christian status of South America. Such summary analyses necessarily give an incomplete picture, and in our case we have underlined the limits of the system; but this does not deny that the system possessed an authentic validity, augmenting the Christian experience and reflection. Indeed, its womb held the seeds of a rebirth of the Church.

In recent centuries one or other of these pillars supporting the Tridentine system have appeared to tremble, but as a whole the system has always survived the various crises which had only brought about certain individual degenerations. Beginning with 1958-1959, through a whole concourse of historical and spiritual factors, and certainly under an impulse of the Holy Spirit, the Catholic Church (and more generally the entire Christian world) abandoned the Tridentine system on all fundamental themes. The brief intervening time cannot distract us from the global dimensions and the definitive significance of this abandonment.

From this angle it is easy to perceive a singular analogy between the beginning and end of Trent and the opening and closing of the fourth centenary. Then, the modifications occurring between 1545 and 1563 were so great as to make the work of the assembly just concluded appear inadequate to cope with the pressing exigencies; now, whereas in 1945 Trent still dominated the life of the Church and constituted its rule of action, twenty years later we must take note of its complete and definitive historicization. The system derived from Trent is superseded by the beginning of a new phase of Christian history. With the conclusion of its "guiding function", the great council will continue to represent a fundamental stage in the history of the Church; without any longer being a norm of action, it will retain a very great interest for historical research[19] which better than before will be able to identify the original contribution both of the council itself and of the system that applied its name to the development of the Christian experience. Now, in fact, the renown and survival of Trent are relegated to the insertion of its original contribution in the great riverbed of Christian tradition. The reversal in question can be expressed as follows: between the second half of the 16th century and the first half of the 20th century the Church's contact with Christian tradition was ruled and screened by Trent. Henceforth, however, the knowledge and influence of Trent will depend upon its assimilation into the Christian conscience.

[19] The celebration of Vatican Council II has suggested a few themes for research pertaining more to the method of work and the organization of the Council of Tent than to the individual arguments confronted by it. Thus H. Jedin, "Die Geschäftsordnungen der beiden letzten ökumenischen Konzilien in ekklesiologischer Sicht," in *Catholica* 14 (1960), pp. 105-18 and *Strukturprobleme der ökumenischen Konzilien* (Cologne, 1963). Always from the methodological viewpoint this would seem to deepen—providing much valuable evidence—the relation between Trent and the implementations of its decision to which we have made some reference above.

Roger Aubert/*Louvain, Belgium*

Religious Liberty from "Mirari Vos" to the "Syllabus"

Liberalism in its different forms, especially religious liberty, was stigmatized by Pius IX as "the error of the century". In this matter he followed the many Ultramontane publicists of the time. In the course of the 19th century liberalism and religious liberty were frequently the object of *monita* or even of formal condemnation by ecclesiastical authorities and, notably, the Holy See.

Two documents, Gregory XVI's encyclical *Mirari vos* (August 15, 1832) and the *Syllabus* (December 8, 1864) accompanying Pius IX's encyclical *Quanta cura,* are prominent among the magisterium's acts because of their frequent use either by theologians or by anti-Catholic polemicists. Although both groups have all too often failed to place these papal documents in historical context, it is important to do so, if we are to grasp their real import and, in particular, their permanent doctrinal significance.[1]

[1] In this article I will draw on my writings on the teachings of the ecclesiastical magisterium in the 19th century as they regard liberalism. These are to be found in the collection (now out of print) *Tolérance et communauté humaine* (Tournai, 1952), pp. 75-103. Cf. "Le Syllabus de décembre 1864," in *La Revue nouvelle* XL (1964), pp. 369-85, 481-99.

I

THE ENCYCLICAL "MIRARI VOS"

The famous encyclical *Mirari vos*,[2] whose title is inextricably linked with the name of Lamennais,[3] the first prophet of Catholic liberalism, was not an encyclical explicitly directed against the liberal system as the encyclical *Quanta cura* of Pius IX was to be thirty years later. It was, in point of fact, the inaugural encyclical of Gregory XVI, postponed for more than two years by the revolutionary disorders that had shaken the Papal States. Presenting a grievous picture of the sad state of the Church at the dawn of the pontificate, it drew attention to three principal dangers: rationalism and Gallicanism, which Lamennais had been denouncing with so much energy for some time, and liberalism. Apropos of this third and without actually naming *L'Avenir* and the persons connected with it, the pope clearly disavowed a certain number of ideas they were advocating.

We may recall, briefly, that under the influence of Lamennais, the French journal *L'Avenir* had initiated a double campaign which attracted a good deal of interest abroad: in favor of the independence of the Church from the civil power (in opposition to Gallican pretensions), and in favor of a free renunciation by the Church of the State's compromising protection enjoyed by the Church. This twofold demand aimed to substitute for the system of a "State religion" and a "privileged Church"—factors that were usual under the *ancien régime*—a new system of separation of the two powers. It was presented in the name of an ideal of liberty that also led Lamennais to attack absolutism and the theory of the divine right of kings, as well as to support the rights of certain national groups (Belgians, Poles, Irish) in their struggle for independence.

[2] Original Latin text in *Acta Gregorii XVI*, ed. Bernasconi (Rome, 1901), pp. 169-74. French translation in *Lettres apostoliques de Pie IX, Grégoire XVI* (Paris: Bonne Presse, 1903), pp. 201-21.
[3] See in particular Dudon, *Lamennais et le Saint Siège* (Paris, 1911). This is a one-sided account but it is still indispensable because of the Vatican sources to which the author had access.

These views, which were in direct opposition to the whole political philosophy of the Restoration epoch and which had been denounced at Rome by several heads of State, with Metternich in the lead,[4] must have been particularly offensive to Gregory XVI. In the aftermath of the uprising in the Papal States in 1830, Gregory XVI was very much aware of the dangers to which liberal agitation would expose the temporal sovereignty of the popes. It was almost inevitable that Gregory XVI, "obsessed with the idea that the Papal States were falling apart under the impact of modern ideas, would confront these ideas with redoubled vigor".[5]

The following are a few particularly characteristic passages:

We come now to a source which is, alas! all too productive of the deplorable evils afflicting the Church today. We have in mind *indifferentism,* that is, the fatal opinion everywhere spread abroad by the deceit of wicked men, that the eternal salvation of the soul can be won by the profession of any faith at all, provided that conduct conforms to the norms of justice and probity. . . .

From this poisonous spring of indifferentism flows the false and absurd, or rather the mad principle that we must secure and guarantee to each one liberty of conscience; this is one of the most contagious of errors; it smooths the way for that absolute and unbridled freedom of thought, which, to the ruin of Church and State, is now spreading everywhere, and which certain men, with outrageous impudence, do not fear to represent as advantageous to religion. But what more fatal blow to the life of the soul than freedom of error, says St. Augustine. As we thus see lifted from the shoulders of men the reins that alone can keep them in the way of truth, dragged as they already are by their natural

---

[4] See L. Ahrens, *Lamennais und Deutschland* (Münster, 1930). The author publishes the correspondence of the Austrian Ambassador to Rome, which was unknown to Dudon.

[5] A. Simon, "Vues nouvelles sur Grégoire XVI," in *Revue Générale Belge* (January, 1951), pp. 399ff.

inclination to evil to the very brink of eternal loss, it is in truth that we say that there now lie open before them the jaws of the abyss, of which St. John spoke. . . .

To this [error] is attached liberty of the press, the most dangerous liberty, an execrable liberty, which can never inspire sufficient horror, and which some men [nevertheless] very noisily and insistently demand [and attempt] to spread everywhere. . . .

Then, after a long exposition of the advantages of the legislation of the *Index*, comes a disavowal of the solution put forward by *L'Avenir*—separation of Church and State:

We cannot foresee any happier results for religion and the civil power from the desires of those who so warmly advocate the separation of Church and State and the rupture of the agreement between clergy and Empire. For it is a well-known fact that all the most ardent lovers of liberty fear more than anything else this concord that has always been as salutary and as fortunate for the Church as it has been for the State. . . .

To interpret intelligently this condemnation of the liberal system through and beyond the curt rigidity and the sometimes disconcertingly swollen formulas of curial Latin, one must take into account different things that will enlighten us on the real thought of the pope, more complex in reality than it may appear at first glance.

In the first place there was no intention at Rome of closing the doors in practice on every instance of "modern liberty", including freedom of worship and of the press. Proof of this is to be found in the fact that at the very moment when the encyclical *Mirari vos* was being written, Gregory XVI not only refrained from disavowing—as some people urged him to do—the Belgian Constitution of 1831, based on these liberties and on the principle of separation of Church and State, but he went further: in spite of certain denunciations he named the Vicar General Sterckx as

Archbishop of Malines. This was the man who had undertaken to justify these principles in Belgium and Rome.[6]

At the same time, it is also clear that Rome very much wanted this system to remain the exception, a second-best. There was no intention of deliberately throwing away the great apostolic advantages that were thought to reside in the system inherited from the *ancien régime,* in which the civil power lavished its favors on Catholicism, a system which, according to circumstances, still remained in force in most Catholic countries, in a more or less total fashion. It was precisely Lamennais' proposal that this state of affairs be everywhere freely renounced, because it was more a hindrance than a help. It was this absolute position that Rome did not want to admit.

Moreover, one cannot take up again the "minimalist" interpretation of certain disciples of Lamennais who thought it was possible to state that the encyclical *Mirari vos* confined itself to blaming *L'Avenir's* propaganda in favor of the new regime of separation; in other words, that it had no bearing on doctrine and was only a disavowal of a policy judged inopportune for the moment because of political circumstances. In fact, the part of the encyclical treating of liberalism had, in the mind of the pope, doctrinal implications. The theological Commission summoned by the pope to examine *L'Avenir* had clearly put the problem in a doctrinal setting and concluded that it was necessary to censure severely the exaltation of popular sovereignty, separation of Church and State, freedom of worship and of the press, because these theories were derived from a certain indifferentism toward faith. The Commission added that it would be good to oppose these theories with the Catholic teaching on the origin of secular authority, the collaboration that the secular arm should give to religion and the social necessity of truth.[7] A second argument is even more conclusive: Cardinal Pacca's letter to Lamennais,

---

[6] Cf. A. Simon, "Le vicaire général Sterckx et la constitution belge," in *Miscellanea Historica . . . L. Van der Essen* II (Brussels, 1948), pp. 983-90.

[7] Dudon, *op. cit.,* p. 177.

pointing out in the pope's name that he saw him in the encyclical, no doubt called attention to matters of strategy, but also signalized points of doctrine.[8]

From this point forward, then, it is possible to say that the Roman position at the moment of the encyclical *Mirari vos* was as follows: toleration of modern liberties is acceptable in cases in which it cannot be avoided and on condition that the rights of the Church are safeguarded. Moreover, it is agreed that where constitutional liberties have been imposed by public opinion, Catholics should place on this foundation the defense of religion and the Church. On the other hand, the proposition that equal rights for all, Catholic and non-Catholic, and freedom to disseminate every kind of teaching represents progress and is an ideal to be aimed at, is formally condemned. On the contrary, such a situation is not, in itself, beneficial.

At the same time, in order to interpret the papal document correctly, two points must be added. First, when the pope condemns liberty of conscience, he twice employs expressions that denote unrestricted liberty; *"plena illa* atque *immoderata libertas opinionum* . . . freno *quippe* omni *adempto* . . ."* We are all the more disposed to admit that it is against this unbridled liberty that the extremely severe strictures of the encyclical are directed when we keep in mind the remark that Gregory XVI was later to make to Czar Nicholas I: "Liberty of conscience must not be confused with liberty not to have a conscience."[9]

The latter expression is much more important for understanding the real meaning of the encyclical. It is obvious that what the document condemns is, above all, an apologia for liberty and liberties that seems to stem from a naturalistic concept of man. Rome unmasked in the concrete liberalism of the period a clear statement of man's emancipation from God and a deliberate rejection of the primacy of the supernatural.

[8] Dudon, *op. cit.,* pp. 194-5. The second and third points are obviously doctrinal.

[9] Cited by A. Boudou, *Le Saint Siège et la Russie* I (Paris, 1922), p. 436.

Certainly the collaborators of *L'Avenir* had not gone so far as this; they were not taking for their own the philosophical bases of the "liberal" system, notably the theoretic indifferentism to which the encyclical claimed to trace it.[10] Quite the reverse was true. But in the overall picture of the period, they were doomed to appear as making concessions to this system, and as taking up positions that would logically lead to it. This was all the more true in that they had not been sufficiently careful to rethink the principles that would allow them, with discrimination and the necessary purification, to assimilate to Christianity the ideas of freedom and democracy which, born outside the Church, had developed in a spirit hostile to her.[11]

II

THE SYLLABUS

Very different from Gregory XVI and less concerned than he was to defend at all costs the legitimist principle dear to the men of the Restoration, Pius IX, who succeeded Gregory XVI in 1846, nevertheless had scarcely any more inclination than his predecessor for liberal forms of government. Above all, he was in total agreement with him in what concerned ideas of Church-State relations.[12] The revolutionary crisis of 1848 and the reaction that followed it in every part of Europe could only confirm him in his mistrust of systems based on modern liberties. In fact, by revealing to what a degree the traditional social order had been shaken, this crisis had once again posed, and with a new

[10] In the name of a logic that did some violence to the complexity of the concrete positions of many of the liberals of 1830. It is well known that this is often the case with ecclesiastical condemnations, which mean to stigmatize the ideas that are judged to be dangerous, rather than to judge the intentions of the men who are propagating them.

[11] On this point, see the judicious remarks of Y. Congar, *Vraie et fausse réforme dans l'Eglise* (Paris, 1950), pp. 345-6, 562-9, 604-22.

[12] On the so-called liberal sympathies of Pius IX in the first two years of his pontificate, see R. Aubert, *Le Pontificat de Pie IX* (Paris,²1963), pp. 14-29, 505-6; and *idem*, "Pie IX et le Risorgimento," in *Risorgimento* IV (Brussels, 1961), pp. 52-8.

urgency, the great problem that confronted the Catholic world since the beginning of the century: the attitude to be taken with regard to a world emerging from the intellectual and political revolution of the 18th century, and, in particular, with regard to the civil and religious liberties proclaimed in the Declaration of the Rights of Man.[13]

The violence of the convulsions that had once again been shaking all of Europe for the past few months, not even sparing the papal throne, could only strengthen in their convictions all those who thought there was a direct relation between the principles of 1789 and the destruction of traditional values in the social, moral and religious order. Henceforth, there were very many among the clergy and the faithful with a traditional cast of mind, who could see salvation only in an authoritarian Catholicism. They sought to keep, or to recapture, for the Church a regime of privilege and of external prestige at the heart of a State officially Catholic, shielded from the pressure of public opinion. More sensitive to the scandal of the weak than to the scandal of the strong, they insisted on the fact that the masses, above all the rural segments of the population, which still formed the vast majority of the European nations, would less easily abandon a Church honored by the secular arm and recognized by it.

Moreover, it was in the name of the new freedoms that the sovereignty of the pope in his own States was being questioned. The Piedmontese government pursued a policy of laicization that not only forced the Church out of areas of public life, which for centuries she had considered hers by right, but also culminated in the expulsion of religious and the imprisonment of priests. This left the field open to Protestant propaganda, the effects of which were to be dreaded particularly in the Italy of the Risorgimento.

In these conditions, it is easy to understand the concern of many responsible churchmen faced with the growing sympathy

---

[13] Typical from this point of view is his inaugural encyclical *Qui pluribus* (November 9, 1846), or the allocution *Ubi primum* (December 17, 1847).

for liberal ideas to be found in certain Catholic circles.[14] They were all the more disturbed in that, conservative as most of them were and instinctively attached to the past, they had great difficulty in distinguishing between the eternal verities that must be maintained at any price and the contingent structures of the ecclesiastical or civil order. Besides this, they were deeply impressed by the fact—and it was a very impressive fact about 1860—that wherever the liberals were in power, they had hastened to pass legislation hostile to the Church.

Placed as he was at the center of Christendom, the pope was obliged to lend a ready ear to the violent representations of all who pressed him to speak out clearly and without equivocation. At the same time various factors were combining to reinforce his own fears: the increased movement of many Italian Catholics toward "conciliatorist" positions; new measures against convents in many countries of Europe and America; Protestant propaganda in Latin America, the influence of which was heightened by the vast distances and the inadequate preparation of the masses to resist it; the success in France of Renan's *Life of Jesus* and/or the atheistic philosophy of Littré, which made men look back with regret to "the good old days" when governments, enjoined by the Church, proscribed non-Catholic proselytizing and the sale of "bad books".

All this alarming news succeeded in convincing Pius IX that liberalism, the synthesis of the 18th-century Encyclopedists' philosophy, recast in a political form by the French revolutionaries, was truly "the error of the century", an error he was duty-bound to condemn once again by drawing the attention of Catholics to all the forms—sometimes subtle ones—that this tendency could assume in the concrete. Its aim would be to free man from the intellectual and moral obligations that are the normal result of the supernatural revelation given to him. In many cases he was able to recognize the practical necessity men felt of tolerating the constitutional governments based on these famous "modern liber-

[14] On the whole context, see R. Aubert, *Le Pontificat de Pie IX* (Paris, ²1963), Chap. VIII, and notes, pp. 531-37.

ties", and even the use which might be made of them in certain cases to assure the Church maximum freedom of action. The pope also believed that in spite of their good intentions certain liberal Catholics, especially in France and Italy, too easily sided with the prevailing situation. He felt that they were going too far in making concessions to it, and more and more were running the risk of passing from a "practical" attitude to a doctrinal adhesion to the naturalist and indifferentist principles. In his eyes, this constituted the ideological basis of liberalism.[15] Therefore, a serious warning seemed to him to be increasingly necessary. This warning was to be the *Syllabus* and the encyclical *Quanta cura,* of which the *Syllabus* was only an appendix—an appendix that would, moreover, catch the attention of the public much more than the encyclical itself.

The two documents, in preparation since 1859,[16] were published in December, 1864, They were presented as a summary of the principal modern errors that Pius IX had already sketched in his allocutions *Singulari quadam* (1854) and *Maxima quidem* (1862). The encyclical[17] denounced in rather general terms the pretensions of the State to suppress religious congregations and to monopolize in its own name the education of youth; the royal power, inherited from Gallicanism and Josephism, which requires authorization by the civil power for the exercise of ecclesiastical authority; the claim that the decrees of the Holy See are to be obeyed only in what concerns matters of dogma while inde-

---

[15] On the difference between the liberal *Weltanschauung* and the position of many Catholic liberals, see the very balanced remarks of A. Simon, "Considérations sur le libéralisme," in *Risorgimento* IV (Brussels, 1961), pp. 3-25.

[16] On the preparation of the *Syllabus,* see in particular C. Rinaldi, *Il valore del Sillabo, Studio teologico e storico* (Rome, 1888), and G. Martina, "Osservazioni sulle varie redazioni del Sillabo," in *Chiesa e Stato nell' Ottocento, Miscellanea P. Pirri* II (Padua, 1962), pp. 419-524.

[17] *A.S.S.* 3 (1865), pp. 161ff. French text in *Lettres apostoliques* (Paris: Bonne Presse), pp. 3-17. See English text in Anne Fremantle (ed.), *The Papal Encyclicals in Their Historical Context* (New York: G. P. Putnam's Sons, 1956), pp. 135-43; Lancelot Sheppard (ed.), *Twentieth Century Catholicism* (New York: Hawthorn Books, 1965), pp. 142-53.

pendence can be maintained in matters of discipline; the radicalism of the exegetes who considered Christ as a myth or who denied his divinity. Finally, and above all, it denounced naturalism that sees progress in the constitution and government of human society without reference to religion, and that would henceforth claim as ideals the secularization of institutions, the separation of Church and State, freedom of the press, the equality of sects before the law and total liberty of conscience.

To this encyclical was added a catalogue of 80 propositions that were declared unacceptable, entitled *The Syllabus of the Principal Errors of Our Time*.[18] Here were to be found the principal modern errors that Pius IX had been condemning over and over again in his allocutions and encyclicals for the past fifteen years, those which had just been mentioned in the encyclical *Quanta cura* and a few others: pantheism and materialism; rationalism, which holds that the Christian faith is opposed to human reason, or which at least for philosophers claims a complete independence with respect to revelation; and for the theologians the freedom to work without taking account of the decisions of ecclesiastical authority. Also included were erroneous moral concepts concerning Christian marriage, socialism that would subject the family in its totality to the State, the theoreticians of liberal capitalism who considered the organization of society to have no other end than the acquisition of wealth, and also attacks on the temporal power of the papacy.

In fact, the encyclical and the *Syllabus* accompanying it grappled with a large number of theological, philosophical, canonical and practical matters. But, from the time of their publication and in the period since then, these documents have attracted attention principally because of one facet of their character

---

[18] *A.S.S.* 3 (1867), pp. 168ff. or Denzinger, 1700-1780. The best commentary on the *Syllabus* is that of L. Choupin, *Valeur des décisions du Saint Siège* (Paris,³1928), pp. 187-415. See English text in Anne Fremantle (ed.), *The Papal Encyclicals in Their Historical Context* (New York: G. P. Putnam's Sons, 1956), pp. 143-52; Lancelot Sheppard (ed.), *Twentieth Century Catholicism* (New York: Hawthorn Books, 1965), pp. 12-60, 154-64.

which had received special development: the position adopted with regard to the system of modern liberties, of liberalism in theory and in practice.

The encyclical itself was scarcely read outside ecclesiastical circles, shielded as it was by the grandiloquent style that put it safely out of public notice. But in the *Syllabus,* the same trenchant and brief teachings appeared, easily accessible to the uninitiated. Never, perhaps, has a papal document made such a stir in secular society, and, in certain circles, never has one produced such a scandal. Many men saw in it the solemn and decisive confirmation of the incompatibility of the Catholic Church with the 19th-century habits of thought and modes of life. And many Catholics, especially in France and Belgium, anxiously asked themselves if they had not been driven into a corner where they would have to break with the Church in order to remain men of their own time.

In fact, it was inevitable that the solemn intervention of Pius IX against liberalism would have a much greater repercussion than the encyclical *Mirari vos* had had in 1832. Not that the position of the latter with regard to liberalism had been any more conciliatory; quite the contrary. We must remember three things. First, when he condemned liberalism in 1832, Gregory XVI was responding to the wishes of the majority of the ruling classes, reactionaries in most countries, for whom liberals were just so many incorrigible children. But in 1864 the *Syllabus* took up a position that was clearly against the mainstream of public opinion. Secondly, in the thirty years since 1832, the papacy, as a result of the progress of Ultramontanism, had acquired with the Church a leadership that was much more important than any it could lay claim to at the beginning of Gregory XVI's pontificate. A declaration from Rome in 1864 was binding on the universal Church and on ecclesiastical circles in each country in a much clearer way than was the case in 1830. Finally, we may add the fact that pressure from one part of the clergy and the faithful, very well organized against Catholic liberalism for a few years past, obliged the bishops even reluctantly to give greater emphasis to the new papal document than they had given to Gregory's encyclical. We should realize, for example, that in 1832 the Belgian episcopate gave no publicity to *Mirari vos* because they considered it a document written by theologians for theologians. In 1864, on the contrary, it was inevitable that discussion would be carried on in the public forum, with all the risks of misunderstanding and exaggeration which that entails.

These risks were particularly great for a document like the *Syllabus*—in the first place because it presented, in haphazard fashion, errors and even heresies and formulas that were simply clumsy or imprudent. The papal Secretary of State drew attention to this point in private audiences; the general public knew nothing about it. Nor was the public aware of the classical rule that when we are faced with a proposition censured by the Church's teaching authority, in order to know the positive teaching of the Church in the matter, we must take the contradictory of the proposition and not its contrary, as one is naturally tempted to do. Finally and above all, the *Syllabus* constituted a case that is probably unique in the history of papal interventions: it was, in fact, made up of extracts from earlier documents of Pius IX, and it was carefully stated that, in order to understand its precise meaning, reference should be made to the documents from which each of the propositions had been drawn. In certain cases, this operation is most enlightening—for example, the famous proposition 80, so astounding on first reading, since it seems like a repudiation of those who hold that "the pope should effect a reconciliation with liberalism, progress, and modern civilization". As a matter of fact, in the allocution of March 18, 1861, from which the proposition in question had been quoted, the pope cried out against those who demanded that he make his peace "with what they call modern civilization and liberalism", pointing out that behind these words there lurked in reality laws against convents, harassments of priests who remained faithful to the pope, support of the Church's enemies, etc. He concluded: "If, by the word *civilization* must be understood a system invented on purpose to weaken, and perhaps to overthrow, the Church, never can the Holy See and the Roman Pontiff be allied with such a civilization!" Obviously, there are fewer problems here.

Unfortunately, if the accompanying letter of Cardinal Antonelli stated in explicit terms that the propositions of the *Syllabus* were to be interpreted in the light of the previous papal documents from which they had been taken, these documents were obviously not available to everyone who read the propositions in the newspaper with their morning coffee. Moreover, even the interpretation of these documents often called for weighing the meaning of the technical terms employed, or required general propositions to be distinguished from particular statements. And all of this needed no small store of theological subtlety, of which very few laymen, and even few of the clergy, were capable. We have here a particularly striking example of the remarkable absence of any sense of public relations, so often urged as a reproach—and quite rightly—against ecclesiastical authorities and against the Vatican in particular. They frequently fail to bear in mind that documents officially destined for ecclesiastics —supposedly well armed with all the resources of classical logic, scholastic theology, and canon law—will inevitably enter the public domain and be read by the unsophisticated who are going to understand the terms in their current sense. They do not take into account a certain number of important reservations that are not laid down in black and white but are simply presupposed by the experts.

It must be added that this undue "inflation" of the import of the papal pronouncement was not attributable solely to the lack of expertise on the part of the average reader. It is equally attributable to certain Ultramontane polemicists, who, taking the wish for the fact, were in their turn tempted to understand certain of the propositions in the desired sense, without any concern for their actual context. They too quickly came to the conclusion, on reading the *Syllabus,* that all their own anti-modern prejudices had been canonized by Rome. For example, the organ of the Spanish Traditionalists—echoed, it must be said, by the principal journal of the French Ultramontanists, *Le Monde*—wrote: "Our unique faith is henceforth to stigmatize liberalism, progress and modern civilization as anti-Catholic. We condemn as anti-Catholic these abortions of hell."

In the face of interpretations as excessive as these, which were picked up by the anticlerical press the better to ridicule the papal intervention, it is not to be wondered at if, at first, many people thought that the pope had repudiated all the modern constitutions based on the principles of 1789 and on the recognition of the fundamental liberties. At the very least, many thought that the teachings of the "liberal" Catholics were now condemned by the Church. The well-known bishop of Orleans, Bishop Dupanloup, who occupied a conspicuous position as one of the inspirers and one of the most representative of the group, succeeded nonetheless within the space of a few days in bringing the situation back to normal by a skillful commentary that replaced the propositions of the *Syllabus* in their context, and interpreted them in the light of the distinction between *thesis* and *hypothesis*.[19] Truly, this soothing commentary met with nothing but praise, and, even among the bishop's friends, many, though they rejoiced at the results he obtained, were only half convinced. One of these was Montalembert, who wrote to the bishop: "I am one of those who feel that you have switched the babies, and, as the *Journal des Débats* has it, that you make Pius IX bless Jacob instead of Esau." Certainly, there was a good deal of dexterity in Dupanloup's pamphlet. But it must be recognized that the benign interpretation of the papal documents it proposed was much less of a distortion of the pope's thought than people were led to suppose in certain circles.

From the point of view of practical applications, first of all, it is incontestable that Rome never considered going back on the acceptance in fact of the constitutions based on the recognition of modern liberties, even if this recognition went, as it did in

[19] See R. Aubert, "Mgr. Dupanloup et le *Syllabus*," in *Revue d'histoire ecclésiastique* 51 (1956), pp. 79-142, 471-512, 837-915.

Belgium, as far as the legal separation of Church and State. Repeated assertions from the Secretary of State and from Pius IX himself in succeeding weeks clearly showed that in the mind of the Holy See neither *Quanta cura* nor the *Syllabus* intended to change anything in the attitude of toleration-in-practice that had been previously adopted.

But what was the state of the question in theory? It is important to note that in *Quanta cura,* even more clearly than Gregory XVI in *Mirari vos,* Pius IX represents the different freedoms he has condemned as stemming from "the impious and absurd principle of naturalism", and from a viewpoint that refuses to admit a difference between the true religion and others. Further, in the *Syllabus* the section that most nearly concerns our subject bore the title: *Errores ad liberalismum hodiernum pertinentes:* Errors connected with *contemporary* liberalism. It was, therefore, less a question of the essence of liberalism *per se* than of the form in the concrete that the liberal system was taking at the period, and even more, perhaps, of liberal practice. The liberalism contemporary with the *Syllabus,* as it was being expressed by its leaders and the methods of the liberal governments in power practically everywhere in continental Europe and Latin America, quite often became militant anticlericalism and meddlesome control of the life of the Church. Sometimes it even went so far as to try to strangle her by real oppression, with the idea, very widespread at the time, that religion was an obstacle to human progress. Even when liberalism did not go to these lengths and remained faithful, not only in words but in deeds, to the ideal of religious freedom, 19th-century liberalism usually laid claim to religious freedom in the name of a purely relativist concept of religions, stating within a framework of indifferentism that it was because all religions have more or less value as the human expression of religious sensibility that all of them must be accorded full liberty. If the formula "A free Church in a free State" had none of this relativistic and naturalistic meaning for Montalembert—and Pius IX realized this though he regretted some of the Frenchman's rather equivocal expressions—it certainly had this meaning in the mouth of Cavour and for the many liberals who thought as he did. Pius IX knew this, too. It was especially against this brand of liberalism that he intended to strike a blow. It was normal that a pope, responsible for the integrity of the Christian faith, would clearly condemn such indifferentism, naturalistic in its inspiration.

Once we have said this, we must add that Pius IX also intended, in the name of a certain anthropology current in the traditionalist Catholic circles of his time, to strike at a liberal organization of society. Not everything in this attitude was false. It had an obscure presentiment of what was defective, socially and economically, for those outside the privileged leaders in such an organization. It is nonetheless true that it implied a systematic distrust with regard to democracy, and it is in this area that the intervention of Pius IX is outdated. It is this area in which a slow maturation of Catholic thinking has had as its consequence a progress in doctrine, reaching from the encyclicals of Leo XIII, through certain of the discourses of Pius XII and the declarations of *Pacem in Terris,* to the Schema on Religious Liberty presented at Vatican Council II. But, while we recognize that side by side with the reminder of certain principles that have permanent value and timely admonitions, there is in the *Syllabus* more than one statement that belongs to the past, or that drew its inspiration from a system of political philosophy in which the Church today no longer recognizes its deepest thought, it is nonetheless an honorable undertaking to try to understand why Pius IX was led to take up such a position, apparently so anti-modern.

It is possible to realize, by a rapid review of the situation in 1860, that it was much more for religious—or more exactly, for pastoral—reasons, than for political or social reasons. Historical research, then, has not solely the result of allowing us to understand better the exact meaning of papal documents; it goes further, to help us to interpret validly certain papal interventions that can appear particularly disconcerting to the uninformed observer today.

Jacques Fontaine/*Paris, France*

Christians and
Military Service
in the Early Church

The events through which we have lived during the last quarter of a century have revived a fruitful but dangerous interest in the attitude of the first Christians toward war and military service. Both pacifists and defenders of the "just war" have reread the texts of early Christian authors, often with an untoward emotionalism, in order to justify their own bias. This is the more regrettable as the evidence itself is emotionally inspired, fragmentary, literary and bound up with local situations and conditions that are difficult to reconstruct in their concrete circumstances. The objective interpretation of these texts and the exact determination of the authors' purposes are difficult enough by themselves. How much more difficult should it not be to use these texts correctly in order to solve our own problems in this field?

That is why I shall refer only briefly to the shorter articles which do not pay enough attention to the historical problem involved, and are often written under the influence of excessively modern prejudices: occasional studies that embroider upon a few classical texts from Tertullian, Hippolytus or Origen.[1] Nev-

---

[1] Such an article was the short and hesitant study by F. Schulte on "Tertullianus en de Krijgsdienst," in *Onder eigen Vaandel* 12 (1937), pp. 71-89, written under the emotional impact of the threat of a war shortly to break out. It was communicated to me by my friend, the Rev.

ertheless, I have selected, though not exhaustively, some studies made by historians, scriptural and patristic scholars and theologians, which invite personal reflection and occasionally open up new and original perspectives on this question. These will be examined in chronological order.

A good collection of texts and facts can be found in R. H. Bainton's article, "The Early Church and War".[2] In it he shows the complexity, contradictions and gaps in our documents. He insists persuasively on the growing diversity of functions which saddled the Roman army, particularly from the Severi onward and even within the structure of the *militia armata:* this great diversity of responsibilities, entrusted to troops that were more and more specialized, made it possible for Christian soldiers to continue in the service without having to shed blood. This factor makes some statements by Hippolytus and Tertullian less paradoxical. It also invites us to study the problem, so to speak, from within the Roman army, and not only from the point of view of the Christian communities.

This is why the article by the specialist on "conversion" and hermetism, A. D. Nock, "The Roman Army and the Roman Religious Year",[3] is more than a mere digression in this discussion. This study, which appeared in 1952, goes beyond the simple analysis of the religious calendar of the XXth cohort stationed at Palmyra, a document (ca. 225), discovered at Doura. He not only shows that this *Feriale* "was not exclusively

---

Golliet, professor at the University of Nijmegen. To this same group belong: H. Minn, "Tertullian and War. Voices From the Early Church," in *The Evangelical Quarterly* 13 (1941), pp. 202-13, meditative in style, written during the war, based on a defective collection of texts and translations with little comment; the anti-pacifist article by H. Davis, "The Early Christian Attitude to War," in *Blackfriars* 30 (1949), pp. 477-82, written in postwar America, and the recent controversy between G. S. Windass (pacifist position) and the Rev. J. Newman (anti-pacifist reply) under the title "The Early Christian Attitude to War," in *Irish Theological Quarterly* 29 (1962), pp. 235-48.

[2] R. Bainton, "The Early Church and War," in *Harvard Theological Review* 39 (1946), pp. 189-212, reprinted in the symposium *The Church, the Gospel and War* (New York: R. Jones, 1948).

[3] In *Harvard Theological Review* 45 (1952), pp. 187-252.

religious and did not contain the whole of a soldier's religion",
but also that preoccupation with a loyalist liturgy coexisted in
the Roman army of the 3rd century with much true liberalism.
The army kept aloof from religious quarrels, and this situation
changed only when the tetrarchy demanded a personal religious
obedience of every soldier. This article has the appeal of a historical, quasi-sociological reflection upon the military profession
and upon the religious problems peculiar to the military mind.
Concentrating on the concrete reality of life in the army, it com-
plements and widens the overly narrow perspective likely to
result from an exclusive concentration on literary texts produced
by convinced Christian scholars, rhetoricians and philosophers,
however great their reputation in the field of early Christian
literature.

The year 1952 also saw the appearance of an article by E. A.
Ryan: "The Rejection of Military Service by the Early Christians".[4] Clearly but without exaggeration, the author distin-
guishes three main phases in the problem before the peace of
Milan. In actual fact the problem does not arise before 170.
The increase in the number of Christians, the growing importance of local recruitment (when the Empire was threatened by
the Marcomani), and lastly the worship of the emperor as *do-
minus* confronted Christian soldiers with problems of conscience
which were no longer isolated instances.

The first to witness an awakening of conscience to the seriousness of the problem, among both pagans and Christians, were
Celsus and Tertullian. Not, however, till the second half of the
3rd century did the military and imperial authorities abandon
tolerance for open and systematic persecution. While the article
clearly shows the evolution of the data of the problem, it also
draws a distinction between the theory adopted by the writers
and the attitude of maintaining the *status quo* adopted by the
majority of Christian soldiers to whom the Church gave no explicit directive that would demand a change of attitude. Thus
the writers remained confined within their theoretical doubts,

[4] In *Theological Studies* 13 (1952), pp. 1-32.

while the soldiers found a *modus vivendi* that was not necessarily of a questionable character. Consequently, it becomes
still clearer how necessary it is to discern the changes in the
historical context as well as a certain shift of emphasis between
the reflections of the authors and the real life of the soldiers.

The same need for such a distinction is no less emphasized by
H. von Campenhausen's study on "Christian Military Service in
the Early Church".[5] More aware of the legal and ideological
factors, he shows how the early Christians did not seem interested in the problem during the early Empire when conscription
was unknown, and that this lack of interest can be explained
more in general by their indifference toward political responsibility. The strictness of the canons of Hippolytus corresponds to
that of Tertullian, but the works of Clement of Alexandria show
a more liberal and more finely qualified attitude. Only Origen,
anxious to find an answer to pagan criticisms, is led to formu-
late "a basic political judgment" by asserting that a Christian
should accept civic responsibilities but utterly refuse to shed
blood. But how far can one accept, with the author, that Origen's kind of pacifism is due much more to a late Platonic
spirituality than to the Bible? It is true that a current of pacifism
runs through the later phases of Stoicism, as some texts of
Seneca clearly show, but that certain anti-militaristic statements
of Tertullian and Origen are inspired by a radical evangelism
seems a fact difficult to deny.

Granted, however, this hardly contestable fact, it is not so
easy to establish whether we have to deal here with a purely
personal extremism (even though the person is a teacher or
cleric), or whether we should recognize in Tertullian's teaching
an "echo of the Church's discipline". This is the line taken by
J. Daniélou, perhaps a little hastily, in his brief synthesis.[6] The

---

[5] Hans Freiherr von Campenhausen, "Der Kriegsdienst der Christen in
der Kirche des Altertums," in *Festschrift K. Jaspers* (Munich, 1953),
pp. 255-64 (reprinted in the coll. *Tradition und Leben* (Tübingen, 1960),
pp. 203-15).

[6] J. Daniélou, "La non-violence dans l'Ecriture et la tradition," in *Action chrétienne et non-violence* (Paris, 1955), pp. 9-32.

most interesting section of this brief study treats the influence of certain Old Testament texts on early Christian thought concerning military service (*militia*), particularly Is. 2, 1-6 and 50-53. Equally rich in teaching for the early Christians was Christ's attitude toward the zealots and toward Jewish nationalism. O. Cullmann, too, in his small but compact book, *The State in the New Testament*,[7] clarifies indirectly, on the basis of the New Testament, the principles that should guide all Christian thought on the State and on its recourse to violence in certain cases. As shown in the Gospels, Christ's attitude is one of tension, allowing the State what is necessary for its existence, but on condition that it does not interfere with what is due to God. Paul and John are equally coherent and in harmony with their master's position, if one reads Romans 13 as referring to the first half of Christ's statement while the reinforced imposition of the emperor's cult explains the judgment and violent condemnation of the State in the Apocalypse.

Another perspective on the problem, though converging toward the same previously mentioned apocalyptic dualism, is opened up by José Capmany's study on the soldier of Christ in the spirituality of St. Cyprian which also appeared in 1956.[8] The title vaguely recalls Harnack's famous brief study. But insofar as Capmany deals much more fully with all the aspects of this theme in Cyprian, his study leads to a deeper reflection on the implications of a spirituality based on the "spiritual militia" in the service of Christ, and on the motives that inspired the attitude of Christians in the 3rd century toward the *militia Caesaris*, the service of Caesar. This whole spirituality, indeed, as Cyprian lived and preached it, was linked with the possible or actual test of martyrdom. The systematic persecution of the days of Decius and Valerian gave a tragic actuality to the great vision of the apocalyptic duel. Violence appears there at the

[7] O. Cullmann, *Dieu et César* (Paris, 1956), English ed. (SCM, London, 1963).

[8] J. Capmany, "Miles Christi en la espiritualidad de San Cipriano," in *Collectanea San Paciano*, Serie Teologica 1 (Barcelona, 1956).

service of the Prince of this world (with or without a capital letter). The soldiers (*milites*), particularly those belonging to the imperial police troops, imprison and execute the martyrs. Parallel to this view, the development of the baptismal liturgy certainly gives the *signatio* and the *sacramentum* the features of a conscription into the ranks of Christ's army, as opposed to the army of the persecuting emperors. One may wonder whether the imagery and ideology of spiritual service and combat did not sublimate natural aggressiveness to a point where the evangelical demand for nonviolence and for a break with the world would be felt much more deeply.

The years 1957 and 1958 saw the appearance of two comprehensive studies which, in spite of their difference in scope and theological background, show nevertheless what might be called a common ecumenical tendency in the rather small field of this inquiry. For these two German studies, one by the Evangelical theologian H. Karpp, the other by the Catholic B. Schöpf, have many qualities in common: sound information, thorough analysis, the refusal to simplify, respect for persons and facts, the wish to understand before judging and to overcome still too common clichés by more careful judgment. Karpp's closely argued article on the position of the early Church with regard to military service and war,[9] contains some remarkable views which affect the methodical interpretation of texts and facts. First of all, one must realize that the Christian position changed according to time and place. Christian soldiers stationed on a threatened frontier like the Euphrates could hardly look at the problem with the same academic detachment as a professor at Alexandria or a cleric at Carthage or Rome. One should therefore understand that the problem was first of all a live one, and had to be solved according to the demands of the concrete situation. This is a simple truth which a screen of literary texts might obscure. In his excellent pages on Tertullian the author takes care to put the texts on the *militia* in the context of Ter-

[9] H. Karpp, "Die Stellung der Alten Kirche zu Kriegsdienst und Krieg," in *Evangelische Theologie* 17 (1957), pp. 496-515.

tullian's general refusal to share any responsibility or to have anything in common with the pagan State. He shows that these texts "express a demand and do not describe an attitude", and that Tertullian's conduct throughout shows a "tension" (*Spannung*—the author does not say "contradiction"). These two observations are particularly relevant for the interpretation of Tertullian's volatile and enigmatic texts.

Perhaps one should go still deeper into this matter. We ought to try to give greater precision to the meaning of that "demand" in relation to the literary genre of so many moral treatises of Tertullian. His preaching is still closely connected with the classical literary genre of the diatribe. As such its style is hyperbolical and his use of exaggeration and rhetorical contortion would deceive his first listeners and readers much less than most modern readers. Tertullian is too often seen through the eyes of the Holy Office when people try to assess theologically the exact degree of his inclination toward heresy throughout a series of works whose chronology is difficult to establish. One should look on him, first of all, as a man of letters, a kind of Christian Apuleius. One may therefore well ask whether, by rhetorical self-intoxication, he did not end up with believing literally his own formulae. For they were, to start with, so many paradoxical *sententiae,* and at least in the extreme cases, were employed as Tacitus used them in his *Agricola* against the imperialism of Rome. Moreover, this literary view should be complemented by a philosophical one, and the "tension", laid bare by Karpp, demands the examination of a way of thinking which today we would call "dialectical".[10] But here we should, of course, avoid the ill-suited generalizations beloved of Hegel. One should therefore begin with the contradictory statements which the practice of *controversia* demanded of Roman writers. Moreover, Tertullian's way of arguing is the more difficult to grasp, for it is constantly interfered with by legal, dialectical and rhetorical habits

[10] It will soon be possible to see this aspect of Karpp's theological reasoning in P. Moingt's thesis, *La Théologie trinitaire de Tertullien,* to be published this year by Aubier, Paris.

of thought without mentioning the indirect but powerful influence of thoughts and expressions inherited from the diatribe of the Pauline Epistles.

The final section of Karpp's work reassesses the change in 313 with a prudence which is far from common among theologians of all denominations. For him, the Church of Constantine was not immediately aware of the dangers implied in the new situation, and "took a truly historic decision in an unusual and unexpected situation". Here again, the gradual change in the Christian attitude toward the *militia armata* must be seen and judged in the concrete situation, and not approved or condemned on the basis of abstract norms or texts of a much later period.[11]

The same intellectual adroitness and the same respect for the concrete situation mark the work of Bernhard Schöpf, in spite of the apologetic tendency admitted in the preface.[12] His first care is to widen the horizon of the problem by extending it, on the one hand, to the general problem of the "right to shed blood", not only in war but also in executions, murder and games of the amphitheatre, and on the other by starting his inquiry with a detailed outline of scriptural precedents and the background of pagan thought. Thus he locates the problem within ancient civilization as a whole without isolating the Christians within their little spiritual ghetto. In contrast to the justification of war and the progressive development of the notion of a just war in Greek classical philosophy, the few anti-militarist and anti-imperialist texts of Seneca analyzed by Schöpf are particularly helpful in putting Tertullian's most outrageous statements in their true light. Both bear witness to the continuity of certain traditional themes of the diatribe from paganism to Christianity.

In the chapters devoted to war, the author establishes the striking difference between the evidence of the literary tradition

---

[11] This is still the case, unfortunately, in Newman's reply to Windass (see note 1), since he begins by quoting a text of St. Augustine's which he then proceeds to apply to the centuries before Augustine.

[12] B. Schöpf, *Das Tötungsrecht bei den frühchristlichen Schriftstellern.* Studien zur Geschichte der Moraltheologie, V (Regensburg, 1958). For our subject, see ch. 10, "Der Krieg," pp. 198-240.

and what he calls "the attitude of the Christian people and the Church". Thus he separates this attitude from that of the great Christian authors, both Latin and Greek, Hippolytus included. The careful examination of all the "non-magisterial" documents, enriched by epigraphy, the study and dating of the earliest *Acts* of the military martyrs, and the understanding of Christianity as lived in the army (cf. certain letters found among the papyri of the Abinnaean Archives in Egypt), gives us a more correct notion of the Christian attitude toward the *militia*. The author cautiously concludes that there was a slow development of Christian thought on problems whose intellectual content became clear only very gradually. After 313 there was no "gradual secularization" but rather "a cautious and prudent adjustment to the secular order willed by God".

The delicate approach of these two studies stands in sharp contrast with the impassioned book of J. M. Hornus on the Gospel and the imperial standard, published in 1960.[13] It reads like a colorful and blunt antithesis of Tertullian. And that is what it intends to be, more or less. In spite of the honest intention to collect a historical dossier of the problem, it is a systematic work, more concerned with deduction than with a careful assessment of the infinite diversity of both documents, and men of various generations and regions of the Empire. The dangerously abstract and prejudiced character of the book is clear from the very headings of the chapters: "The Political and Social Framework", "The Ideological and Religious Framework", "The Christian Attitude", "Christian Soldiers and Military Saints", "Christian Anti-militarism as the Official Attitude of the Church".

The documentation is rich but not adequately criticized, dated or arranged in distinct chronological phases—different in this respect from practically all the works mentioned above. It is a vast storehouse of references, but the construction is shaky.

---

[13] J. Hornus, *Evangile et labarum. Etude sur l'attitude du christianisme primitif devant les problèmes de l'Etat, de la guerre et de la violence* (Geneva, 1960).

There is a fair amount of naïve criticism, particularly in the careless use of 4th and 5th century texts on "military martyrs". These texts are so elaborate, stylized and rewritten that their historical value is much more difficult to assess than their contribution to our knowledge of Christian spirituality at that time.[14]

This peculiar work will remain a mine of texts and references for French readers, but they will have to beware constantly of the interpretation and coherence of the whole argument. The extensive and methodical bibliography seems to me one of the most important collections on this question. It is, unfortunately, lacking in scientific objectivity and the ancient texts have been conscripted into a misdirected crusade. They have not been examined with the respect, method and patience necessary to get at their true meaning.[15]

Anna Morisi's book on the war in Christian thought from

[14] I have pointed out one of the best examples of this in my article, "Sulpice-Sévère a-t-il travesti Saint Martin de Tours en martyr militaire?" in *Analecta Bollandiana* 81 (1963), pp. 31-58, where I have shown how, in the *Vita Martini*, there is a romantic account of Martin's defiance of Emperor Julian.

[15] Two articles by the same author, one published before, the other after the appearance of his book, must be mentioned. His "Etude sur la pensée politique de Tertullien," in *Revue d'Histoire et de Philosophie religieuses* 38 (1958), pp. 1-38, is much better and more objective than his book. It is an interesting attempt to show how Tertullian tried to argue from what the opposite consequences of Romans 13 and Apocalypse 13 would lead to. He also shows the wavering of the Severi in religious affairs, and how the emphasis changed gradually in Tertullian's writings under the influence of the persecutions which drove the Christian out of the world he tried to live in. The careful description of Tertullian's drift toward a heterodox rigorism is worth quoting: "Tertullian lost his grip in the subtle dialectic of a day-to-day love of the sinner and a total hatred of sin." One regrets that the author did not rewrite some harsh pages of his *Evangile et labarum* in this prudent vein. The same author's article, "L'excommunication des militaires dans la discipline chrétienne," in *Communio viatorum* (1962), pp. 41-61, forms a kind of appendix to the book, and reflects the same dogmatism. How far can the Canons of Hippolytus, the rigorist anti-pope, be taken in the form in which they have reached us as reflecting the Church's discipline without any further qualification? And how can one speak of *one* discipline of the Church at such an early date and particularly on such very controversial questions—*quaestiones vexatissimae?*

the beginning up to the crusades,[16] is no doubt more objective but also written in more haste, and the very scope of the period covered—over a thousand years—makes one feel uneasy about it. A whole millennium promenades before the reader's eyes in barely two hundred pages. Even though the author limits herself to a study of the development of ideas in Christian authors and to a commentary on the basic texts, this interesting study remains, nevertheless, too sketchy. There is no indication of the preliminary problems in Judaism, the New Testament, Jewish Christianity, nor of the ancient pagan tradition. The liberalism of Clement of Alexandria is said to be the "true position of the Church" as opposed to the "heretical extremism of Tertullian". Such conclusions are rather oversimplified and dangerous in that they lead one to believe that there could be *one* clearly defined position of the "Church" at the beginning of the 3rd century on a problem still so obscure in the conscience of the majority of Christians. The book shows a sound sensitiveness with regard to the texts of Tertullian, but, pressed for time, the author has concentrated the conclusions of her chapters in a way that makes them suspect.[17]

Taking all these studies together, one has the impression that, with few exceptions, there has been progress in objectivity, in careful discretion with regard to the texts, in the awareness of the difficulty of understanding men and situations in the concrete, and in the desire to listen intelligently to what others have to say instead of drowning their voices in personal prejudice. Henceforth it will be difficult to collect and to publish ingenuously a dossier of one-sided quotations for pacifist or anti-pacifist

---

[16] A. Morisi, *La Guerra nel pensiero cristiano delle origini alle crociate* (Florence, 1963).

[17] I have not been able to consult the book by W. Dignath Düren, *Kirche, Krieg, Kriegsdienst. Die Wissenschaft zu dem aktuellen in der ganzen Welt* (Hamburg, 1955), nor R. Bainton's *Christian Attitudes toward War and Peace* (New York, 1960). Nor have I been able to find E. Molland's article in Norwegian on the Christians and military service in the early Church, which appeared in *Norsk Teologisk Tidsskrift* 60 (1959), pp. 87-104.

propaganda, as it used to be done at the beginning of this century. This is not to say that the shifting complexity of successive historical situations should reduce us to a silent skepticism, confronted as we are with contradictions between various authors or within the thought of a single author. On the contrary, in an age when the dialectical progress of modern thought has taught us to get beyond the static logic of Aristotle, it is encouraging to see that even in those far-off days and in spite of the less perfect intellectual means (particularly in the Roman world) the truth was sought by means of a dialogue between contradictory demands, between the "discipline" so dear to Tertullian, and the pressing situations of life itself.

These situations varied according to individuals and generations and even from year to year. It has been rightly emphasized in connection with Tertullian how steadily alternating tolerance and persecution must have weighed on the Christians' attitude toward the State of Rome under the Severus dynasty, and, consequently, on the concrete way in which they accepted military service. It will no longer be so easy to state without qualification that Tertullian's voice is that of heretical extremism or of the Church's tradition, when he declares that no Christian can lawfully accept military service.[18] One will have to distinguish carefully between his apologetics and his exhortations, and see Tertullian's genuine attempt to be faithful to both Romans 13 and Apocalypse 13, the conservative and perhaps even archaic element in his clearly stated reasons and hidden motivations, and above all, the hyperbole typical of the man of letters, and the concrete situation within which he wrote each of his treatises. The problem must be carefully followed from one generation to another, from one region to another (a man from Alexandria does not argue like a man from Carthage); it must be seen in the light of the social situation of the army and the increasing importance of the military in all the activities where it gradually

---

[18] This was still done by A. Morisi (*op. cit.,* n.16) and J. Daniélou (*op. cit.,* n.6).

ousts the civilians in the period approaching the later Roman Empire.[19]

Only on this condition can we understand, profit by, and learn from, the Christian attitude toward military service during the first centuries and after the peace of Constantine when the labarum was marked by the cross. It would be laziness and contrary to the Christian mentality of the time to dream in a stoic and nostalgic fashion of a return to the purity of Christian sources. Heinrich Karpp put it very well at the end of the article he wrote in 1957: "The early Church decided according to the situation in which she found herself. We simply cannot adopt the decision which was hers. It is up to us to make our own decisions, with all the seriousness required, on the basis of our present and past historical experiences." The Christians of the first centuries did not live in an atomic age. But their voice can still remind us of the demands of the Gospel to which the situation of today lends urgency. This voice can help us see our own problems and enlighten "The Conscience of the Christian and Nuclear Weapons", as Cardinal Charles Journet did with such scrupulous care a year ago.[20]

[19] This is why R. MacMullen's stimulating little book, *Soldier and Civilian in the Later Roman Empire* (Cambridge, Mass., 1963) leads to fruitful reflection in this field although it does not explicitly deal with the religious aspect of his theme. I have mentioned this in my review of it in *Revue des Etudes Latines* 41 (1964), pp. 500-1.

[20] This is the title of his distressing and demanding article in *Nova et Vetera* 39 (Fribourg, 1964).—In conclusion I would like to thank all those who have helped me to make this article less incomplete, particularly the editors of the *Dictionnaire de spiritualité* at Chantilly, my friend Pierre Petitmengin, librarian of the Ecole Normale Supérieure, and my colleague and friend, H. I. Marrou.

PART II

BIBLIOGRAPHICAL
SURVEY

Anton G. Weiler/*Nijmegen, Netherlands*

Church Authority and Government in the Middle Ages

Vatican II has incorporated the principle of collegiality in its constitution *De Ecclesia*. Connected with this there has been talk about an apostolic papal council, a permanent body for advice and liaison composed of members of the world's hierarchies organized to assist the pope in the central government of the Church as a kind of prolonged "Council". All this makes a historian take another look at the Middle Ages. Attempts were already made during that period to devise a theory and practice of extended collegial co-responsibility which acquired a new shape in the 20th century. Moreover, the general atmosphere of Vatican Council II allows the historian the freedom to assess in a more positive manner some historical phenomena that he had learned to eschew or reject through a too narrow understanding of Vatican Council I.

This shift in historical perspective, brought about by contemporary developments and the progress of historical research, becomes evident when we compare, for example, the dogmatic undertones of Walter Ullmann's *The Origins of the Great Schism*[1] with contemporary discussion of the dogmatic signifi-

---

[1] For a discussion of this work (London: Burns & Oates, 1948) see, among others, E. de Moreau, "Une nouvelle théorie sur les origines du Grand Schisme d'Occident," in *Bulletin, Classe des Lettres,* of the Académie Royale Belge, 35 (1949), pp. 182-9. J. Leclercq, "Points de vue

cance of the fact that Pope Martin V approved the decrees of the Council of Constance.[2]

Ullmann's work brought no new facts to light but he went back to the sources to discover the factual and alleged reasons why in 1378 the cardinals after a few months dropped their first choice, Archbishop Bartholomew Prignano of Bari (Urban VI), and substituted Robert of Geneva (Clement VII). It became clear again, as Yves Congar has already pointed out,[3] that the resulting division in Christendom was not really a schism. There was no break with the Church's teaching. There was no heresy which drove a group of Christians out of the *Una Sancta*, dividing the faith by rejecting the pope. The point at issue was rather which of the two elected rivals was the true head of the one, universal and inviolate Church.

Ullmann, however, stressed the deeper causes of the conflict between pope and cardinals by interpreting the schism as a constitutional crisis within the Church. Not the person of the pope but his function within the whole hierarchy of the one universal Church was being queried. Since the end of the 13th century papalist authors and theologians such as Aegidius Romanus, Augustinus Triumphus, James of Viterbo, Alexander à S. Elpidio, Alvarez Pelagius and others, pushed further and further with their radical and hierocratic papalism. They tried to condense the function of the whole Church into the function of the

---

sur le Grand Schisme d'Occident," in *L'Eglise et les Eglises,* II (Chevetogne, 1955), pp. 223-40, is mainly concerned with the religious importance of the schism, which, according to the author, deserves to be called "Great" because of the great stimulus it gave to reflection on the unity of the Church and the indivisibility of the papal office. See also the most recent study of this theme by K. Fink, "Zur Beurteilung des Grossen abendländischen Schismas," in *Zeitschrift für Kirchengeschichte* 73 (1962), pp. 335-43.

[2] I refer here to A. Franzen's article on the Council of Constance in the present issue of *Concilium,* which contains an extensive bibliography. See also the recent, handy, well-written but bibliographically poor study by J. R. Palanque and J. Chelini, *Petite histoire des grands conciles* (Présence chrétienne, Bruges: Desclée de Brouwer, 1962), where the meaning of Martin V's ratification of the council is discussed in Chap. III, 16, pp. 153-6.

[3] *Dictionnaire de Théologie Catholique,* 14 (1939), p. 1295.

pope who had the plenitude of power, could not be judged, could not be deposed and was infallible.[4] At last the cardinals came out in protest against this theory which became the practice at Avignon[5] when it tended toward centralization and absolutism. Ullmann sees in their reaction the rise of a new concept of the Church. By "Church" they meant the one college of pope and cardinals. On the basis of the oligarchic concept they claimed control over the pope.[6] The pope was not entitled to govern arbitrarily but was bound to govern in union with the other members of the college. As the cardinals, however, were unable to solve the crisis provoked by themselves, this control shifted, as the schism persisted, from the college of cardinals to the community of the faithful, represented by the General Council. Thus conciliarism represented a second and more penetrating reaction against an exaggerated papalism. The democratic idea broke through in the Church.

No doubt, such ideas about the governmental structure of the Church reflected the tendencies of an age when political corporations and social groups tried to maintain their rights over against a similar absolutism in kings and governors of town and country.[7] The constantly increasing assertion of political thought

[4] Apart from the studies by Ullmann, Tierney and Wilks, mentioned later on, which contain extensive bibliographies, I refer to J. Moynihan, "Papal Immunity and Liability in the Writings of the Medieval Canonists," in *Analecta Gregoriana, LXX, Series Facultatis Iuris Canonici*, sectio B, n.9 (Rome, 1961), who examines particularly the question "whether or not a pope can be made to stand trial before an ecclesiastical tribunal" (pp. IX-X). His investigation covers the period from 500 A.D. to the teaching of Cardinal Zabarella inclusive. The decisive period is that between 1140 and 1220, from the *Decretum Gratiani* to the *Glossa Ordinaria* of Johannes Teutonius. It deals with a great quantity of unpublished matter from various *Summae* of that period.

[5] A detailed picture of social life at Avignon may be found in B. Guillemain, *La cour pontificale d'Avignon, 1309-1376. Étude d'une société* (Bibl. des Ecoles françaises d'Athènes et de Rome, Paris, 1963).

[6] The latest study of this subject is that of J. Leclerq, "Pars corporis papae. Le Sacré Collège dans l'ecclésiologie médiévale," in *L'homme devant Dieu. Mélanges Henri de Lubac*, II (Paris, 1964), pp. 183-98.

[7] The various studies by G. Post have recently been collected in *Studies in Medieval Legal Thought. Public Law and the State, 1100-1322* (Princeton, 1964). The many publications on political thought, mainly

in both Church and State since the second half of the 11th century has been the subject of an uninterrupted series of studies,
partly stimulated by ideas about the corporate State in the years
before World War II.[8] According to Ullmann the critical aspect
of the schism lay in that the ecclesiastical laws in force during
that period were incapable of showing a way out of this constitutional impasse. "The pope cannot be judged by anyone unless
he is found to deviate from the faith" (*Papa a nemine iudicatur,
nisi deprehendatur a fide devius*), is the rule laid down in Gratian's *Decretum*.[9] But in this case there was no question of heresy. Ullmann therefore not only thought the cardinals' action
illegal but considered that their oligarchic concept of the Church's
government was contrary to the faith, anti-dogmatic. He found
it a "strange phenomenon" [10] that these leading figures of the

English and American, are mentioned in this volume. Most important are
the 5 volumes of G. de Lagarde's *La naissance de l'esprit laïque au dé-
clin du moyen âge*, of which a new and up-to-date edition has been published by Nauwelaerts, Paris-Louvain: Vol. 1: *Bilan du XIIIème siècle*,
3rd ed., 1956; Vol. 2: *Secteur social de la scolastique*, 2nd ed., 1958;
Vol. 3: *Marsile de Padoue* (3rd ed. being prepared); Vol. 4: *Guillaume
d'Ockham: Défense de l'empire*, 1962; Vol. 5: *Guillaume d'Ockham:
Critique des structures ecclésiales*, 1963. Volumes 4 and 5 have not appeared before. Although the literature and sources examined by de
Lagarde have not been collected in separate surveys, one can form
a good idea of this material by means of the excellent indices of authors
quoted and of names and subject matter.
  [8] One might refer to the series of studies under the title of *Standen en
Landen* (*Anciens pays et Assemblées d'États*), published since 1937,
where full attention is given to the different forms of the corporate State.
The much quoted article by G. de Lagarde, "Individualisme et corpora-
tisme au moyen âge," in *L'organisation corporative du moyen âge à la fin
de l'ancien Régime*, Vol. 2 (Louvain, 1937), pp. 1-59, is closely connected with the ideas of "solidarism" of the 'thirties, and investigates
whether the supporters of the corporate idea of those years were entitled to base themselves on the medieval philosophy of a corporate society and state. The author's preference for modern corporate ideas,
however, has repeatedly affected his historical judgment.
  [9] D. XL, c.6. Moynihan, *op. cit.*, pp. 25-42, has devoted a whole chapter to this text. See also B. Tierney, *Foundations of the Conciliar Theory*
(Cambridge, 1955), pp. 57ff. and App. I, pp. 248-50. More will be said
about this work.
  [10] Ullmann, *op. cit.*, p. 183; see also p. 187. The introduction to the book
shows at once the dogmatic position from which Ullmann starts.

Church let themselves be guided by ideas that ran contrary to the dogma of the primacy. Ullmann completely backed St. Thomas's formula (*Summa Theol.*, IIa IIae, a. 39, 1)[11] according to which the unity of the Church is brought about not only through the association of the Church's members among themselves but also through the subordination of all members to the one Head, Christ, whose exclusive *vicarius* is the pope.

In Ullmann's later works, too[12], we find the notion that, according to what he calls "the teleological principle of functional qualification", the divinely instituted papacy was bound to lead to a form of government of the monarchical type. By this divine institution the pope possesses an all-powerful jurisdiction. According to Ullmann the historical process from the 5th to the 15th centuries led straight from biblical and specifically Pauline teaching to principles of government of a hierocratic nature, and since Gregory VII these principles were embodied in concrete acts of government. The bishops' share in the primacy waned. Institutionally there was no room in the Church for contract theories based on Roman or medieval law, or for ideas about the supreme sovereignty of the people as propounded not only

[11] Ullmann, *op. cit.*, pp. 183ff.
[12] In his *Medieval Papalism. The Political Theories of the Medieval Canonists* (London: Methuen, 1949), pp. 18ff., Walter Ullmann examines the period from the second half of the 12th century to the end of the 14th century. But this study, too, suffers from the doctrinal preconceptions that have already been referred to. The critical study by A. Stickler, "Concerning the Political Theories of the Medieval Canonists," in *Traditio* 7 (1949-1951), pp. 450-63, gives an appreciative analysis of Ullmann's work but points out in detail his methodological and ideological errors. Ullmann's *The Growth of Papal Government in the Middle Ages. A Study in the Ideological Relations of Clerical to Lay Power* (London: Methuen, 1955), pp. 42ff., in particular can no longer be used without comparing it with the detailed critical study by F. Kempf, "Die päpstliche Gewalt in der mittelalterlichen Welt. Ein Auseinandersetzung mit Walter Ullmann," in *Saggi storici intorno al papato. Miscellanea Historiae Pontificiae*, XXI (Rome, 1959), pp. 117-69. The same idea that the divine institution of the primacy must necessaily lead to a totalitarian form of government, rightly called a piece of very doubtful theology by Kempf, provides the basis for Ullmann's *Principles of Government and Politics in the Middle Ages* (London, 1961), of which the first part is entitled "The Pope" (pp. 27-115).

by jurists but also, under the influence of Aristotle, by the Italian Averroists (Marsilio of Padua) and the nominalists of the school of Ockham. The idea that the pope should be obliged to rule in agreement with one or other controlling body, whether the college of cardinals or a general council, is, according to Ullmann, in conflict with the Church's dogma.[13]

This final negative judgment, particularly insofar as it contains no qualifications, is certainly dominated by a traditionally too exclusive conception of the primacy. But it is also due in large part to the fact that in the 'forties not enough was known about the rich canonical literature of the Middle Ages. Ullmann's sources were not very representative and too limited in number to do justice to the many opinions which were current before and during the schism about the structure of the Church's government. Since then much new material has been brought to light and investigated, although not yet completely published. The valuable and penetrating studies by A. Stickler, S. Kuttner, Fr. Kempf, M. Maccarone, F. Mochi Onory and particularly Brian Tierney[14] have brought a much better understanding of the medieval canonists, Decretists and Decretalists. These studies have been excellently collected in Tierney's main work, *Foundations of the Conciliar Theory*,[15] which explored particularly the till then inadequately known historical background of legal thought during the period of the schism. In *The Contribution of the Medieval Canonists from Gratian to the Great Schism* Tierney has provided a synthesis. The work clearly establishes that canonists and theologians drew on a vast ancient Catholic heritage of thought which was revitalized during the crisis and prepared for practical use in government.

Tierney's research shows that already in the 13th century the

[13] A survey of recent historical bibliography about the papacy may be found in R. Folz, "La papauté médiévale vue par quelques-uns de ses historiens récents," in *Revue historique* 81 (1957), pp. 32-63.

[14] For bibliography see B. Tierney, "Some Recent Works on the Political Theories of the Medieval Canonists," in *Traditio* 10 (1954), pp. 594-625; idem, "Pope and Council: Some New Decretist Texts," in *Medieval Studies* 19 (1957), pp. 197-218.

[15] See footnote 9.

doctrine developed that authority in a society or other social body cannot be concentrated in the head to the exclusion of the members, but that authority is rooted basically in the community itself. Thus it was held that an ecclesiastical head, too, whether abbot, bishop or pope, could not act without the consent (*consensus*) of the members of the body (*monasterium, capitulum* —chapter—or *ecclesia;* this last term can refer either to the *ecclesia romana* or to the *ecclesia universalis*). The head represents the community not as the personification of the community and its rights, but by the actual delegation of the community's sovereignty. This delegation takes place through the election to which the members give their consent either explicitly or silently.

Tierney points out that these ideas are scattered among the commentators on the *Decretum* (Decretists) and on the papal *Decretales* (Decretalists): they are not worked out into a coherent doctrine. But they are wholly orthodox and fit in with the then prevailing principles of law and with the history of the councils. At the period of the schism, however, oligarchic or democratic tendencies coalesced into a basically constitutional concept of sovereignty in the Church. In the desire to restore under one head the broken ecclesiastical unity, the unity of the faithful, intact in spite of the schism, came more and more to the fore. Since subordination to one head could in fact not function as a constituent of unity, because there were two, and after Pisa, even three "heads", the *congregatio fidelium,* the community of the faithful, came to be recognized as the constituent of unity.

The community, indeed, is one in the faith and the sacraments, even if there happens to be no head. The God-given privilege of never falling away from the faith rests with the community, even if the head were to err. Conciliarism, as the ultimate consequence of the unsolvable situation created by the schism, deprives the pope of his position as the exclusive cornerstone of unity. Like all the faithful he is subject to the council, which represents the community, in matters of faith, unity and reform. The fundamental power is vested in the community, and it is ultimately of little importance whether the basic rights of the Christian community are represented by the college of cardinals, or the general council of the bishops, or a highly democratic gathering, such as that which took place at Basle in 1431,[16] where theologians and laity were given a vote.

The formula which canonists and jurists had already applied for a considerable time to the growing number of semi-autonomous corporations,[17] was adapted to the whole Church in the emergency situation created by the schism. The legalistic tendencies prevailing in the late medieval Church had, however, a double edge. The papalist Decretalists and theologians of the Augustinian school as well as the more moderate Decretists and Thomists used this conception which was derived from Roman law. In their hands it led to a consolidation of both theories, that of an exclusive papal monarchy and that of a constitutional limitation of papal rights. The fact is that legalistic thinking prevailed in both camps and that ecclesiology dwindled into a matter of politics.

Partly relying on earlier and generally accepted studies like those by H. de Lubac[18] and E. Mersch,[19] E. Kantorowicz[20] showed convincingly that this trend of thought led from the

---

[16] There is a very interesting chapter by P. Ourliac, "Sociologie du Concile (de Bâle)," in A. Fliche and V. Martin, *Histoire de l'Eglise. L'Eglise au temps du Grand Schisme et de la crise conciliaire (1378-1449)*, Vol. 14 (Paris: Bloud and Gay, 1962), pp. 237-50.

[17] In his "Studies on the Notion of Society in St. Thomas Aquinas I. St. Thomas and the Decretal of Innocent IV *Romana Ecclesia: Ceterum*," in *Medieval Studies* 8 (1946), pp. 1-42, I. Eschmann collected a long list of names under which medieval ecclesiastical and secular corporations are mentioned in the sources. He did this in a study of St. Thomas's teaching about a corporate criminal offence. The study is interesting in view of the discussions since the last World War about collective guilt.

[18] *Corpus Mysticum. L'Eucharistie et l'Eglise au moyen âge. Etude historique* (Paris: Aubier,[2]1949).

[19] *Le corps mystique du Christ. Etudes de théologie historique*, Museum Lessianum, Sect. théol., Fasc. 28-9 (Louvain, 1933).

[20] *The King's Two Bodies. A Study in Medieval Political Theology* (Princeton, 1957).

originally liturgical and sacramental concept of the Mystical
Body to the sociological reality of Christ's Body, the Church,
whose institutional aspects received most attention to fit in with
the juridical categories of "corporatism". Stickler[21] applied to
this the name *Corpus Christi juridicum*. The Church whose
unity had been seen as based on the eucharist, then became a
regnum ecclesiasticum (ecclesiastical kingdom), a *principatus
ecclesiasticus, apostolicus* or *papalis* (an ecclesiastical, apostolic
or papal principality). The emphasis shifted from Christ as head
of his own Mystical Body to the pope as head of the Church's
Mystical Body (*corpus ecclesiae mysticum*). The final stage of
this totalitarian thinking was reached when the community of
the faithful was made to coincide with the "head". The traditional, patristic and Carolingian view which linked the *eucharist*
to the Church as cause and effect, as means and end and as sign
and signified reality,[22] was pushed into the background to make
room for a view which concentrated on the relationship between
the *pope* and the Church in this respect.[23] A formula was even
found to explain that the Church was the mystical body of the
pope, nay, that the pope *was* the Church.[24] By applying the

[21] A. Stickler, "Der Schwerterbegriff bei Huguccio," in *Ephemerides
Juris Canonici* 3 (1947), p. 216.

[22] De Lubac, *op. cit.*, p. 23.

[23] "Corpus Christi mysticum ibi est, ubi est caput, scilicet papa": Alvarez Pelagius, *Collirium*, p. 506 (ed. R. Scholz, *Unbekannte kirchen-
politische Streitschriften aus der Zeit Ludwigs des Bayern (1327-1354)*,
Vol. 2 (Rome, 1911-1914); quoted by Kantorowicz, *op. cit.*, p. 204 and
Wilks (cf. footnote 24), pp. 31-2.

[24] M. Wilks, *The Problem of Sovereignty in the Later Middle Ages.
The Papal Monarchy with Augustinus Triumphus and the Publicists*
(Cambridge Studies in Medieval Life and Thought, New Series, 9,
[Cambridge, 1963], p. 37). See the excellent reference index under
"corpus papae", "Ecclesia (as Pope)", and "Pope (= Ecclesia)". The
background to the comparable notion of "L'état c'est moi" has been
dealt with in detail by G. Post, "Status regis," in *Studies in Medieval and
Renaissance History* (Univ. of Nebraska Press, vol. 1, 1964), pp. 1-
103. In the course of this study Post has promised a separate study of
the concept of *status ecclesiae*. This has already been undertaken by J.
Hackett, "State of the Church. A Concept of the Medieval Canonists,"
in *The Jurist* 23 (1963), pp. 259-90.

passages in Ephesians 5 about the marital relationship of hus-
band and wife, it was then taken as an automatic conclusion
that the body of the Church must be subject to the head.[25]

In order to understand the growth of Church and society (or
State) in the post-medieval period it is most important to see
that the sources show how these ecclesiastical totalitarian ideas
which grew out of a one-sided interpretation of corporate
thought, namely, the emphasis on the function of the "head"
in the community, became the basis of all secular totalitarian
thought.[26] One has but to think of the "leader" (Führer, Duce)
principle of the fascist and corporate theories of the period before 1940, not to mention more recent illustrations of this form
of government. We can see these ecclesiastical, sociological and
organological ideas, covered by the concepts of *corpus ecclesiae
mysticum* and *corpus papae mysticum*, reflected, for instance, in
English political theory under the Tudors and Stuarts: the *respu-
blica* appears as the mystical body of the king who has universal
jurisdiction over it.[27]

It is, then, obvious that the corporate ideas operated not only
in the sense of conciliarism but also in that of papalism. Some
authors, like Augustinus Triumphus, turned the Church's corporate entity into a concentration of power in the head. M. J.
Wilks has some very revealing pages on this in his extensive and
excellently documented book, *The Problem of Sovereignty*.[28]
He has completed the work of Tierney and Kantorowicz by
bringing to light again the work of the radical-papalistic authors,

[25] J. Trummer, "Symbolik der Ehe und ihre Bedeutung in der mittelalterlichen Kanonistik," in *Im Dienste des Rechtes in Kirche und Staat,
Kirche und Recht,* Vol. 4 (Vienna, 1963) pp. 271-88.

[26] Kantorowicz, *op. cit.,* p. 207. Cf. Wilks, *The Problem of Sovereignty,*
p. 41.

[27] Apart from Kantorowicz's work already mentioned, see also an article
by the same author, "Mysteries of State. An Absolutist Concept and Its
Late Medieval Origins," in *Harvard Theological Review* 48 (1955), pp.
65-91, which is very relevant to this discussion.

[28] (Cf. footnote 24). There is an extensive bibliography on pp. 560-77,
a well selected index on pp. 578-619, and a useful bio-bibliographical Appendix III: "Notes on the Publicists and Anonymous Works," on pp.
548-59.

and by supplying, most sensibly, the logical and historical coun-
terpart of their theses. He brings out the part played by the
radical-democratic authors and the more moderate Thomist supporters of the *via media* in this conflict of ideas. According to
Wilks the authors' reaction to the fundamental philosophical
question about the reality or unreality of universal ideas is basic
to their theories about the State and the Church (as institution).[29] This distinction is more relevant than that proffered
formerly by M. Grabmann,[30] who classified political systems on
the basis of theories about the relationship of faith and reason.
Wilks gives us the following picture. Ultra-realism in philosophy
(Platonism, Augustinianism and, *mutatis mutandis,* Wyclifism)
leads to over-emphasis of the unity of Church or State, represented by the "head" as the principle of that unity, at the expense of the component parts which are totally subject to the
unity subsisting in the head. Nominalism leads to radical democracy, and even individualism, and here there is no unity in
Church or State beyond the members who compose it; hence
the "head" has no authority except by commission from below,
never as the personification of a nonexistent unity. Moderate
realism (Thomism) looks for a middle way and leads to a harmonious unity of head and members on the lines of a constitutional monarchy.[31]

[29] Wilks, *op. cit.,* p. 17: "The constitutional theories of the age were
no more than an expression in terms of government of all the discordant
elements in contemporary philosophy."
[30] M. Grabmann, "Studien über den Einfluss der aristotelischen Philosophie auf die mittelalterlichen Theorien über das Verhältnis von
Kirche und Staat," in *Sitzungsberichte der bayerischen Akademie der
Wissenschaften,* Phil.-Hist. Abteilung (Munich, 1934), Heft 2. This
work is quoted by Wilks, *op. cit.,* p. 17, n. 1, but without referring to the
basic historical criticism of Grabmann's division by A. Gewirth, "Philosophy and Political Thought in the Fourteenth Century," in *The Forward
Movement of the Fourteenth Century,* ed. F. Utley and others (Ohio,
1961), pp. 125-65.
[31] In part I, *The Universal Society,* Wilks compares the *societas chris-
tiana,* the *societas humana* and the *via media;* part II examines the origins of political authority according to the corresponding political view:
the sovereign prince, the sovereignty of the people and the development
of the constitutional monarchy. These theories apply to the pope as well

Lastly, it is striking that Wilks's analysis shows repeatedly that even the most extreme papalistic authors maintain the idea of communal sovereignty as an essential ingredient of hierocratic theory, although in a much less prominent way than in the case of the much maligned Marsilio of Padua. Even Augustinus Triumphus needs the Aristotelian ideas about the natural development of the State and the concomitant ideas about the communal origin of authority in order to preserve the papacy, sublimated to unattainable heights, from finding itself with a heretic or other undesirable on the throne of Peter. Such an undesirable person remains ultimately subject to the judgment of the Church, i.e., of the general council. The communal idea remains operative.[32]

This leads us, naturally, to the great 15th-century thinker, Nicholas of Cusa, who is attracting more and more attention.[33] He developed a new theory of government in which he wanted to give to that community of the Church (and of the State respectively) the place which it ought to have by divine and natural law. His conciliarist synthesis, De Concordantia Catholica, recently available in a complete and critical edition,[34] is a

---

as to kings. On the strictly ecclesiastical level the "right relationship of powers" is examined in parts IV and VI. Part IV, entitled Vicarius Christi, considers the position of the "supreme governor" and the problem of "episcopal government", while part VI concentrates on the conciliar theory. There is also an interesting study by C. O'Neill, "St. Thomas on Membership of the Church," in The Thomist 27 (1963), pp. 88-140.

[32] M. Wilks, "Papa est nomen iurisdictionis", cf. footnote 24.

[33] The older literature on Nicholas of Cusa can be found in E. Vansteenberghe, Le cardinal Nicolas de Cues (1401-1464). L'action. La pensée. (Paris, 1920) of which an anastatic reprint appeared in 1963 (Frankfurt: Minerva). The more recent literature up till 1961 is gathered in the Cusanus-Bibliographie 1920-1961 (Forschungsbeiträge der Cusanus-Gesellschaft I, ed. R. Haubst, Mainz, 1961). I am not able to give here the literature that appeared on the occasion of the Cusanus Jubilee of 1964.

[34] Nicolai de Cusa Opera Omnia, part XIV of the edition of the Heidelberg Academy. Liber I (Leipzig, 1939); II (Leipzig, 1941); III (Hamburg: Felix Meiner, 1959). The general editor was G. Kallen. A new edition of Liber II has appeared aleady (1964); that of Liber I has been announced, and this will bring the necessary Introduction and Register, which were omitted from the 1939 edition.

grandiose recapitulation of late medieval political thought. He harmonizes admirably the institutional rights of the chosen head with those of the men, by nature free and equal, who make up the community. It is also important to realize that Nicholas is acutely aware of the separation of the Western Church from the Eastern, which prevents the Western Church from identifying itself with the universal Church. It is hardly astonishing that, apart from his theological and philosophical works, his theories about Church and State also draw the attention of scholars.

M. Watanabe[35] and P. Sigmund [36] both have attempted to analyze his thought, the former stressing the historical aspect, the latter the more speculative one. Watanabe is therefore useful for tracing the origins of Nicholas's theory of consent, although much of the material is Nicholas's own since he was steeped in Church history and liked to present his ideas as representing ancient practice. Sigmund throws light on the legalistic antecedents and the tradition of Pseudo-Dionysius which helped Nicholas to shape his theory of unity-in-pluriformity. By referring to later statements made by Nicholas about the unity of pope and Church, Sigmund proves that in abandoning the conciliarist position and joining the party of Pope Eugenius IV, Nicholas did not betray a theory which he had so powerfully defended. But even in *De Concordantia Catholica* the position of the pope was clearly set out and his prerogatives recognized. Nicholas, however, was a man who believed in harmony and he neither could nor would be an extremist on either the conciliarist side or on that of the papalists. His thought on *consensus*[37] tries to recon-

---

[35] M. Watanabe, *The Political Ideas of Nicholas of Cusa with Special Reference to His De Concordantia Catholica*. Travaux d'humanisme et Renaissance, LVIII (Geneva: Droz, 1963).

[36] P. Sigmund, *Nicholas of Cusa and Medieval Political Thought* (Harvard University Press, 1963 or Oxford University Press, 1964).

[37] Two important studies by G. Post must be mentioned: "A Roman-canonical Maxim, 'Quod omnes tangit', in Bracton," in *Traditio* 4 (1946), pp. 197-251 (now also in *Studies in Medieval Legal Thought*) and "*Plena potestas* and Consent in Medieval Assemblies. A Study in Roman-canonical Procedure and the Rise of Representation," in *Traditio* 1 (1943), pp. 355-408 (also in *Studies*). The repercussion of this on ec-

cile the rights of the community with those of the head in such
a way that the balance is preserved in the Church, and he sides
with Pope Hormisdas whom he quotes: "God is there where there
is simple, unperverted consent" (*ibi Deus, ubi simplex sine
pravitate consensus*).[38]

The ideas of Nicholas of Cusa may well come to play an
important part, next to the Thomistic synthesis, in contemporary
thought, even in philosophical, theological and religious aspects
to which I have not referred.

---

clesiastical theory and practice was examined by Y. Congar, *"Quod
omnes tangit, ab omnibus tractari et approbari debet,"* in *Revue historique du droit français et étranger* 36 (1958), pp. 210-59. The changes
of principles of Church government, as shown, *e.g.*, in the history of the
provincial synods in England, have been studied by E. Kemp, *Counsel
and Consent. Aspects of the Government of the Church as Exemplified
in the History of the English Provincial Synods.* Bampton lectures, 1960
(London, S.P.C.K., 1961).

[38] *Ad universos episcopos Hispaniae* (Ep. 25, *P.L.* 63, col. 424); *De
Concordantia Catholica*, pp. 204-5.

Hermann Tüchle/*Munich, W. Germany*

Baroque Christianity: the Root of Triumphalism?

In the Constitution on the Church, Vatican Council II has approved not only a doctrinal Schema but has also revealed a new spiritual and supernatural vision in the Church. The Church as the People of God, the Church in dialogue with the world, the Church of the poor, the pilgrim Church differs greatly from the triumphalism and juridicism of the ecclesiastical stance of the recent past. This new outlook nowhere includes an apologetic rhetoric and parade of power, a feeling of assured victory and self-conscious rigidity. Such attitudes, deplored by many, are often described as "baroque". Thus, that great baroque period in the history of the Catholic Church is noticeably devalued. That time, we are told, is somehow responsible for a regrettable deviation in the Church's self-consciousness, a deviation which must be corrected now, as quickly and as thoroughly as possible.

Historians have not yet had the opportunity to pronounce on this new judgment—or condemnation. In recent years, it is true, the authors of some important works have endeavored to understand more deeply and clearly the nature of baroque Christianity by studying certain great men and achievements of that period. These studies were occasioned by a number of recent anniversaries and jubilees. The year 1956 marked the 4th centenary of the death of the founder of the Society of Jesus in Rome. Significant celebrations in 1963 observed the 4th centenary of the end of the Council of Trent. The year 1563 saw the cornerstone laying of the Escorial and the foundation of the first reformed Carmel by St. Teresa of Avila whose 450th birthday occurs during this year, 1965.

The modern view of the Council of Trent and the results thereof, largely due to the work of Hubert Jedin and others, are extensively treated in another contribution in this volume. The 4th centenary of the cornerstone laying of the Escorial has presented to historians a magnificent jubilee edition, a two-volume work published by Ediciones Patrimonio Nacional. This work, entitled *El Escorial 1563-1963* (Madrid, 1963), gives us an idea of the vast complexity of baroque structure: that enigmatic combination of military power as a foundation, material expense, extremely severe simplicity and glittering pomp, spiritual ideas, the inspiration of artistic genius, deep religious fervor and the "mystery of the king", His Catholic Majesty Philip II. And yet, the many material and spiritual elements are ordered according to a certain scheme. The victories of St. Quentin and Lepanto as well as the unexpected rout of the unconquerable armada were, so to speak, only the occasion for the unique foundation of a church, monastery and royal sepulchre. Homage to the divine majesty was the decisive motive, not thanksgiving to St. Lawrence, the patron saint of the victory at St. Quentin —even though the church, San Lorenzo Real, bears his name.

The Escorial is no monument of victory, no triumphal arch, but a confession of Catholicity born of the Spanish soul. In the solitude of the mountains, vying with rocky giants in the background, there rises this religious testimonial as a symbol of the universalism and of the spirit of the Church of Trent, under a sky wholly unlike the serene sky over the Parthenon. A few years earlier, the maxim *cuius regio, illius et religio* had been made the law of discord at Augsburg, the cause of the splintering of religious power and of the strength of Christian faith. Here, however, in the severe enclosure of the Escorial appears the king's longing for unity, for he did not want to "rule over heretics".[1]

This architecture aims at the expression of spiritual things, at first clearly and soberly, without symbolic frills, but later laden with the full splendor of images and likenesses heavily burdened with meaning, open always to the life of the spirit, of intellect, of faith. God is the intended goal. Eight hours a day are devoted to the eucharistic liturgy and the divine office in the church; the adoration of the blessed sacrament must be continuous, and one hundred monks are constantly employed in this task. Here we have the liturgical answer to the dogmatic pronouncements of Trent.

But God is served not only by worship but also in battle against his enemies, and the field of this battle is scholarship. The library, to which the king contributed 4,000 volumes from his personal collection, is not a display of precious books but an arsenal for scholarly research in the service of the Church, precisely because the seminary exists solely for the education of priests.

The Council of Trent had issued its famous decree about the foundation of seminaries on July 15, 1563. In 1567, when the building was not yet finished, the king received 24, and later 40, young men in the spirit of the conciliar decree, "in order to encourage by his example, the bishops in the execution of the decree". For increased academic studies and instruction the king founded the Colegio de Artes y Teologia which is affiliated with, and equal to, those of Alcalá and Salamanca. The reason given for this action is that the king knows "the power of scholarship for the divine service, the preservation and spread of his holy Catholic faith, and the profit deriving from it for the Christian people". Thus this building, in the words of its charter, was to be an aid "in supporting and preserving these our realms in their holy faith and religion, in peace and justice".

Of course the idea of the Escorial and its execution are not

[1] *El Escorial 1563-1963*, 2 Vols. (Madrid: Ediciones Patrimonio Nacional, 1963).

universally acceptable. Its Spanish character is evident. The "mystery of the king" pervades every courtyard and hallway, and the forms of an all too earthly and heroic style are evident. Elements of the High Renaissance are not lacking. But Philip II was no Julius II or Leo X, a point that George Weise emphasized in his contribution "El Escorial como expresion esencial artistica del tiempo de Felice II y del periodo de le Contrarreforma".[2] These popes believed in the possible coexistence of the Church and ancient Roman greatness revived by the humanists. In the Escorial everything, including the heroic style and the concept of grandeur, points to "his divine majesty", to the Almighty who is exposed on the main altar in order to receive the due honor which the Reformers deny him. How simple and severe are the apartments used by the king in contrast to those in the Vatican! There are three rooms, the largest of which is sixteen feet long and contains three windows; in addition, there is an alcove used as a bedroom and a study with a simple bookcase and a few small tables. The ceiling is simple, the walls are white, the floor is paved with bricks. Here Philip lived not like a king but like a monk of the strictest observance. Such are the remarks of the first historian of the monastery. What a contrast between the king's gestatory chair and his regular chair with supports for his arthritic legs, and between the panelled doors provided by Maximilian II and the later furniture designed after the style of Louis XV!

But the baroque spirit is more evident in the men than in the buildings, apartments and furniture. Ignatius of Loyola, Francis Xavier of Navarre, Teresa of Avila, her spiritual daughters and spiritual director, are all living witnesses to the Christian consciousness of the time. Hugo Rahner, perhaps today's outstanding authority on the subject of "Father" Ignatius, has delineated the spirit of early baroque,[3] beginning with the paternal

---

[2] *Ibid.*, II, pp. 273-96.
[3] H. Rahner, *Ignatius von Loyola Mensch und Theologe* (Freiburg, 1956). See also Leonard von Matt and Hugo Rahner, *St. Ignatius Loyola* (Chicago: Regnery, 1956).

castle of the religious founder down to his tomb with its mysterious inscription: *Pour quoy non?* (Why not?). This motto on the coat of arms in the chapel of the Loyolas is also the Basque aristocrat's motto for life. Consciousness of nobility becomes consciousness of election through baptism after his religious conversion. The ideal of his cavalier youth perdures through his life: *Señalarse,* to distinguish oneself, now in the service of the supreme commander who is Christ. His life is filled with the desire for "more", more likeness to the defamed and crucified Lord, but also more of his honor and domination. It is again the "divine majesty" whose service absorbs Ignatius and his friends. What sort of men were they who always desired to tread the stars underfoot, to live always in God and to die to themselves, to burst the limitations of the world and of time; men who would not hesitate to ambition the impossible nor to embrace the menial, as the inscription on St. Ignatius' tomb reads!

The "more" of Ignatius becomes concrete in the "give me souls", the motto of Francis Xavier. While G. Schurhammer presents his documented life with unsurpassed detail,[4] Rahner describes Francis Xavier as immersed in the incomprehensible darkness of the divine majesty in whose hard service he consumes himself, dying as he did in the poverty of the cross, deprived of all human consolation. They also believed in a squandering, uncalculating expenditure of effort in the supernatural sphere. Graces, miracles, visions, visitations and sacrifices were uncounted. In stealthy silence, Ignatius leaves his companions. "United in their jubilation over the profound sense of their task to win the world for Christ", both Ignatius and his understanding disciple acknowledge the "inscrutable mystery of divine election" as well as the mystery of the "crucified majesty". All temptations to triumphalism are rebuffed by readiness for trifling chores and necessities of everyday life, such as "washing one's own clothes and cleaning the kitchen pots", as the aristocrat

---

[4] G. Schurhammer, *Franz Xaver,* 2 Vols. (Freiburg, 1955-63).

Francis Xavier does on board ship in Lisbon. But on the last page of his letter he declares, "With the help, grace and favor of God our Lord I shall confound the devil in that part of the world". Almost a century later it is rightly proclaimed in his praise, *Deo triumphat in omnibus;* even today he triumphs in all things for God.

On the same day of the same year, Francis Xavier and his master Ignatius were canonized together. Thus their spirit was recognized by the Church as her own. This was done by Gregory XV, the founder of the Congregation for the Propagation of the Faith, a pope in complete accord with these two great Jesuits. Just as Ignatius, not yet informed of the death of his friend, wrote him a letter in which he divided the world from Brazil to the Congo, from Ethiopia to China and Japan, in his design for conquering the whole globe for Christ, so the cardinals of the "Propaganda" divided "all the provinces of the world".

From the first actions of the new Congregation shines forth a hopeful optimism based not on human efforts but on the work of the Holy Spirit who, they thought, had opened the gates for the conversion of heretics and infidels. When the imperial army had struck down the heresy in Bohemia, the Congregation did not recommend tribunals but rather charity, preaching, instruction, admonition, prayer, even fasting, tears and the discipline of scourging for the conversion of the erring. It is in the same spirit that, during the deliberations on the disposal of the former ecclesiastical properties in Bohemia, the word was spoken: The heretics should see from the measures taken that the Church wanted to win their souls, not their possessions.[5] Hence the time had passed when the curia—although it is generally admitted that it had received completely false information about the detailed circumstances—sang the *Te Deum* for the destruction of the Huguenots on St. Bartholomew's night, or gave its blessing and consent to the plans for crushing "the perfidious Jezebel of the North" in answer to her murderous overtures. It was thus

[5] H. Tüchle, ed., *Acta S.C. de Propaganda Fide Germaniam Spectantia* (Paderborn, 1962), pp. 1622-49.

no longer believed that the existence of the one Church could be assured by the use of power and harsh exile.

Together with Ignatius and Francis Xavier, the Spanish nun Teresa of Avila was raised to the honors of the altar. G. Papasogli has written her biography as a life of great adventure, the adventure of a generous soul in her struggle for the blessing and love of the Lord.[6] Again we see the tendency toward the absolute, the striving for the infinite in the girl who convinced her brother that it was worthwhile to do something daring for the Lord, even to become a martyr in order to see God. There is something of the spirit of knighthood desiring to excel yet living entirely on love of the Crucified, and in the transport of this love considering that to lead one soul, even for a moment, to the love of God as more important than the possession of eternal glory for itself.

The Carmelite Efren de la Madre de Dios writes convincingly of the kindred spirit of Teresa and Philip.[7] Both were animated by zeal for places of religious fervor and genuine devotion, the emperor and the simple nun concurring in religious reform. While the king proposes a great program, Teresa struggles to obtain the bull of approval for the foundation of her first reformed convent. As Teresa says in her *Way of Perfection*, we retire into the fortress in order to obtain victory. The battlefield was man's conscience; the object of the victory, not territory but ideals. There was no thought of triumph and victory in the low, poor and bare convents Teresa built and where, barefoot and hidden from the world, she prayed with her spiritual daughters. Visions and graces, even if absent from this life, were not the concern of their lives, but rather service of "his divine majesty" and obedience to the Church. Traveling in obedience she dies, and her last words have the assurance of a conqueror: "In the end, Lord, I am yet a daughter of the Church." Her autographs are preserved in the Escorial, indeed the right place, because there her spirit has found its form and home.

[6] G. Papasogli, *Santa Teresia d'Avila* (Rome, 1952).
[7] Cf. *El Escorial 1563-1963*, Vol. 1, pp. 417-37.

Like a roaring storm, the baroque influence was felt also in Germany, especially in the Alpine regions. Here, it is true, instead of rulers like the Spanish king, there were many small princes, bishops and prelates. The new spirit seized the people. Hence L. A. Veit and L. Lenhart entitle their work, *Kirche und Volk im Zeitalter des Barock*.[8] At the risk of overstepping the boundaries of true devotion, there was an especially warm and happy experience of community with God, Christ and the Church, and a new strengthening of the foundation of the Christian life. The churches built at that time were inspired by the realization that there should be ample space and light to praise and thank God for the graces the faithful received. They were erected not because of the abbots' passion for building, but under the compulsion of eternity. As a mirror reflects the light, so these churches were to receive what was invisible and make it visible. The monasteries connected with them were Teresian "castles of souls" where the monks, faced always with images of perfection, were stimulated in their striving.

Like every other period, the baroque had its own dangers. The disciples and admirers of the heroes of faith and the love of God, proud of their predecessors, thought that the harvest was ripe for gathering in the near future. The *imago primi saeculi* of the Society of Jesus reminds one sometimes of such heightened self-consciousness. The worship rendered to the infinite God was soon made the pattern of the ceremonial with which crowned heads wanted to be celebrated. The baroque cult of rulers found representatives even among the sons of Ignatius. The popes relished the aura of the supernatural. Mortimer's reminiscence about Rome in Schiller's drama *Maria Stuart* shows the overpowering impression this attitude made on the people. Bossuet saw "something divine" in the royalty of Louis XIV.

The other face of the baroque coin was absolutism which, it is true, was cultivated mostly in countries that were least touched by baroque. G. de Reynold cites many proofs of this fact.[9] Some-

[8] Freiburg, 1956.
[9] G. de Reynold, *France classique et Europe baroque* (Paris, 1962).

thing of this absolutistic self-consciousness also affected the Church. Titles, ceremonial, court and etiquette covered inner mediocrity, if not an inner void, for some time. Hollow commands and the illusion of spiritual world power concealed political impotence and insignificance; self-assertion replaced charity, particularly toward other Christians whether in the East or in the West. There was yet another danger. The excessive joy at being redeemed was apt to make the people forget the presence of the cross in the midst of Christendom, not only in the sense that distress and misery caused by constant wars were no real concern, but also in the religious sense, *i.e.*, the uncertainty of salvation and sin, and Christ's mysterious bitter penance for it were sometimes taken lightly; the Church had no task of sanctification but considered itself in secure possession of the goal; again, the powerlessness of hell under the cupola of St. Peter's was considered a guarantee of the continued existence of the temporal forms of the Church's invisible substance; and finally the victories over the Turks were regarded as the absolute triumph of good.

Nevertheless, such failures and deviations cannot be unconditionally credited to the account of the baroque influence. Its attitude and forms of expression are certainly no longer those of our time. But then the Catholic Church of today is also different from the original community in Jerusalem. Romanesque and gothic are considered not only styles of art but also forms of Christian faith and life. These earlier forms have passed away. But does the tree of the Church no longer bear within itself any elements of its earlier forms, or has its vital energy long since exhausted certain structures? Does the Church not bear within itself all cultures not only as spread geographically over the face of the earth but also as existing through future and past time? The legitimate heritage of the baroque period must not be the absolutizing of what is human in Church and State, but the awareness of the absolute character of what is divine; it must be a celebration not of present triumphalism, but of eternal triumph.

PART III

DO-C DOCUMENTATION

CONCILIUM

DIRECTOR: Leo Alting von Geusau
Groningen, Netherlands

ASS'T DIRECTOR: M.-J. Le Guillou, O.P.
Boulogne-sur-Seine, France

René Rémond/*Paris, France*

The Problem of Dechristianization

The Present State of the Problem
and Some Recent French Studies

The very scope of the problem of dechristianization has made it to-day a topic of universal interest. It has not always been so. The first to become aware of it were those who pioneered the apostolate among ordinary people. From them the conviction that this phenomenon was of capital importance spread to the religious authorities. The fact that there is dechristianization is no longer questioned however much one may differ on the causes and remedies. At first the problem was seen as purely practical and mainly pastoral, but recently it has become the object of positive study by sociologists and historians. Dechristianization is not merely a matter of religious history: the variety of what are thought to be its causes and the diversity of its effects show that it is a major element in contemporary civilization, perhaps even a constitutive element. As such it ranks —perhaps for the same reasons—with the spread of political and social democracy, urbanization and industrialization in modern society. The study of dechristianization is, therefore, no longer the narrow preserve of specialists and initiates but produces articles in periodicals of general interest. Thus there

149

appeared in France within a few months of each other two articles which informed a large section of the public of the latest research in this field.[1]

Above all, the moment seems to have come to pool the work done in different branches of science which ignored each other and to synthesize the scattered results. The Congress on Religious History, held at Lyons in October, 1963, marked an important stage in the progress of research. On the basis of a report I made to the International Congress of Comparative Ecclesiastical History in 1963 a wide exchange of views took place among historians of many countries and made it possible for the first time to obtain an overall view of the *status quaestionis* and problems of method.[2]

The objective study of dechristianization demands first of all a *definition* and an agreed terminology: it is important that we use the same basic notions and express them in the same way. On the one hand, we must distinguish between dechristianization, secularization and laicization. These terms no doubt designate phenomena that are closely connected and even overlap in historical experience, but they refer to different degrees and processes in the separation of the religious elements from the civil ones. On the other hand, it is important to fix precisely the bearing of equivalent terms in various languages: because of its universal character dechristianization extends beyond the national framework, and research into its causes demands mainly a comparative approach that presupposes an agreed vocabulary. A good example of this is the international vocabulary laid down

[1] G. Morel, "Déchristianisation," in *Études* (May, 1964), pp. 595-613. J. C. Baumont, "La recherche des causes de la déchristianisation contemporaine," in *Chronique sociale de France* (Dec. 31, 1964), pp. 499-518.

[2] R. Rémond, "Recherche d'une méthode d'analyse historique de la déchristianisation depuis le milieu du 19 ème siècle," in *Colloque d'histoire religieuse* (Lyons, Oct., 1963; Grenoble, 1963), pp. 123-54; for a résumé of the discussion see the special issue of the *Cahiers d'Histoire* IX, 1 (1964), pp. 88-106.

by the Vocabulary Commission of the Catholic Center of French Sociology. A sample of this may be found in an appendix to Jean Chelini's *La ville et l'Eglise* (Ed. du Cerf).[3]

The second stage of this kind of research treats the *measurement* of this phenomenon. Any study of dechristianization implies exact numerical data. On this point religious sociology, which has recently grown at a rapid pace, has collected an extensive and varied documentation: there is not a diocese which has neglected to set up an inquiry into religious practice. For some years annual international conferences have brought together specialists in this recent branch of science, drafted lists of what has been and is being done, formulated common trends and made comparisons possible. From this mass of research it is already possible to deduce certain conclusions of a general character and almost to establish certain laws on the stability or decline of religious practice.[4]

But if the historian is thus indebted to the sociologist, he cannot expect that sociology will provide him with all the documentation he needs. For sociology, however well equipped intellectually to pin down contemporary reality, cannot restore the past. The chains of facts it can trace are too short to allow comparison in time, to chart the various developments and to study the origin of the phenomenon. Now, in order to measure the fact, and still more to interpret and study its causes, we must *go back in time*. The contribution made by actual religious sociology must therefore be supplemented by documentary research into

[3] J. Chelini, *La ville et l'Eglise. Premier bilan des enquêtes de sociologie religieuse urbaine* (Paris, 1958).

[4] There are two basic studies on the fundamental principles and method. The first is by the father of religious sociology, Gabriel Le Bras, and consists of articles published during the last 25 years under the title: *Etudes de sociologie religieuse*, I and II (Paris, 1956). The second is by F. Boulard, *Premiers itinéraires en sociologie religieuse* (Paris, 1954). The reports of the international conferences on religious sociology have been published regularly. The bibliography of the papers read there may be found in the *Archives de Sociologie des religions,* from 1958 on, and in *Social Compass.*

the past. This will have to use sources of great variety: administrative documents which contain indications about the confession of those administered, parochial registers so important to obtain a census of what has been done and of the reception of the sacraments, personal documents, memorials, literary documents. For some dioceses and some social categories of a definite character this type of research has already been undertaken and the results have been brought together, thus providing the historian with a precious source of information.[5]

But one should not neglect all that a shrewd student may glean from books or articles which, at first sight, have nothing to do with the rise and fall of religious practice.

Statistical documentation on religious practice creates a delicate problem for both the sociologist and the historian; how must the data be interpreted? The facts that have been collected refer to actions and gestures of religious practice; they reveal outward conduct. What do they tell us about the conscience and the soul? But dechristianization is not merely a matter of a decline in outward observances; it is just as much concerned with feelings and different mentalities. One cannot simply pass, without qualification, from the level of outward observance to that of the human conscience. The level of religious practice may be deceptive: it is quite possible that dechristianization has effectively taken place in the minds while, outwardly, liturgical practice has remained stable and a certain conformity, more social than religious, has maintained itself. On the one hand, one may observe a religious action, and yet this observation may lack all significance from the religious point of view since it may be no more than a certain conformity to social custom. On the other

---

[5] Among recent studies I mention: F. Isambert, *Christianisme et classe ouvrière* (Paris, 1961); P. Droulers, *Action pastorale et problèmes sociaux sous la Monarchie de Juillet chez Mgr. d'Astros, archevêque de Toulouse* (Paris, 1954); C. Marcilhacy, *Le diocèse d'Orléans sous l'épiscopat de Mgr. Dupanloup (1849-78): sociologie religieuse et mentalités collectives* (Paris, 1963).

hand, one should not lightly conclude from absence of outward practice to an absence of religious sense: the lack of practice may be merely the effect of belonging to a particular class. These observations lead to the methodological conclusion that research must also take account of the quality of religious life, the extent of Christian culture and the vitality of the faith. It must take note of social behavior: faithful adhesion to the principles of the Gospel, the use of money, social justice, attitude toward work. Thus dechristianization is measured at the point where many lines of research, covering all aspects of religious life and life in society, converge.

The reason why this kind of research must extend to so many different aspects is that dechristianization is such a comprehensive phenomenon. One realizes the relevance of this truth at the very moment when one tries to *explain* it: confronted by so many diverse causes, one is bound to admit that the only valid explanation is the one which takes in all these factors together. Research into the causes demands a double line of investigation: in time and in space.

Insofar as going back into time is concerned, since historical experience links causality to the succession of events, research into the causes of dechristianization cannot be separated from the study of its origins. If one could date its beginning this would help the causal explanation. But how far back should one go for this origin? The answer to this question gives rise to two different attitudes.

One group of students considers the phenomenon so old that one may even wonder whether there has ever been christianization. If it were shown that certain regions have never been fully christianized, the word "dechristianization" would completely change its meaning. Taken this way, the problem would simply be turned over to the medievalist and historical investigation would pass to another level. But even if we admit that contemporary dechristianization may be the prolongation of a very old situation in some countries or for some social categories, it has nevertheless certain characteristics which make it special, something which cannot be reduced to past history.

The other group of students stresses the profound originality of the fact of dechristianization. For them there is a point in discovering its origins. The origin may vary from one country to another: France was certainly affected much earlier than Italy; in French Canada it is only beginning now, under our own eyes. Within a single country, too, the beginning may vary according to the social milieu. These brief references show how interesting and fruitful comparative research will be. This is the second line which any attempt at explanation must follow.

By intelligently applying the method of differences, *comparison* can expose false explanations, lay bare common causes and assess the proportionate value of the various elements. This comparison should pursue *three lines of approach*. First of all, one should compare countries: thus, for instance, the comparison of the working class in the vast agglomerations of France with the situation in the Ruhr district or in the south of the Netherlands shows that industrialization is not necessarily a cause of mass apostasy; the inference cannot be made automatically. We shall therefore have to look for other factors which must have combined with the factory and the town. Another example helps us to find certain explanatory elements in our study: in the United States the Irish immigrants who were accompanied by their priests and were organized in national parishes, have on the whole remained faithful to their Catholicism, while the Italians, who arrived individually and were only belatedly joined by their clergy, seem on the whole to have become more dechristianized.[6]

In the second place, this comparison must not be limited to one single religion, but extend itself to several. A comparison between Catholic and predominantly Protestant regions is exceptionally enlightening, subject to the methodical difficulties which arise from differences in the regulation of worship.

[6] F. Houtart, *Les paroisses de Bruxelles (1813-1951)* (Brussels, 1955).

Finally our view would be incomplete if we limited ourselves to the cases of dechristianization only: the cases of religious stability and all the exceptions which have escaped dechristianization should be studied with great care. These last factors will be the more interesting in so far as they concern regions which did not escape the influence of the industrial, urban and technical evolution. More significant still are movements in the opposite direction: a collective return to the faith or religious practice either in a region or in a social and professional category. The elements of a persistent practice, and still more, the fact of rechristianization, are just as important as the symptoms of dechristianization. Observation and reflection must take in the whole of these evolutionary trends.

When one tries to draw some conclusions from the diversity of situations and the variety of monographs—there are only very few that are truly comparative—it would seem that the two most constant and decisive factors which lead to dechristianization are the lagging behind of the ecclesiastical mentality and structure, and the appearance of a new social mentality and structure. These two are really twin expressions of one and the same statement: dechristianization is caused by the *distortion* of the relationship between the *Church and the world,* a distortion which is rendered more acute by the increasing speed of the general evolution.

The Church lags behind. In the matter of the Church's organization, for instance, there is the delay—sometimes a delay of twenty years—between the development of new estates on the outskirts of towns and the erection of new parishes and places of worship. In the interval a whole generation has had time to lose its religious habits and to grow up outside the Church: dechristianization has slipped into the gap left between the old parishes and the new suburbs.[7]

[7] *Idem., Aspect sociologique du catholicisme américain* (Paris, 1958); Y. Daniel, *L'équipement paroissial d'un diocèse urbain: Paris (1802-1956)* (Paris, 1957).

On the level of ideas, religious thought, ill-informed, has also lagged behind and shows some analogy with the disjointing of ecclesiastical institutions: here one might recall the whole intellectual history of the 19th century.

A new society has developed; Christians were late to perceive its newness and to discern its positive values because of some provocation. Two features have drawn more attention than others, and usually they are regarded as primary causes of the dechristianization of the masses: industrialization and urbanization. That dechristianization was a direct consequence of industrialization is so widely accepted that one is tempted to believe that there is here a necessary causal link. Yet, comparative studies suggest that this relation is neither quite so obvious nor so simple. It is not rare that one finds regions which have been industrialized, yet have not lost the faith. And when one tries to link the *factory* to the fact of dechristianization, one discovers that here dechristianization is often influenced by aspects of the situation which are not all essential. In one case it may be the lack of the Sunday rest which helped to destroy religious habits; in another it is a matter of accumulating fatigue; more generally it is the constitution of a new social milieu which the Church has neglected. The same can be said about the presumed effects of town life on religious practice[8]: the factory and the town have not brought about dechristianization by a force of their own but rather by the upheaval they have caused in collective habits. Faith and religious practice were part and parcel of a whole system of life and thought: industrialization and urbanization did not attack Christianity deliberately and directly; they first upset and then ruined the traditional social order; by breaking up the social, economic and cultural framework their action ricocheted on religion. Clearly the two types of explanation mentioned above meet: the gravity of the new situation lies in the failure of

[8] J. Labbens, *L'Eglise et les centres urbains* (Paris, 1959); J. Chelini, *op. cit., supra* n.3; J. Folliet, "Les effets de la grande ville sur la vie religieuse," in *Chronique sociale de France* 4 (1953), pp. 539-66.

religion to adapt itself to the change. Thus the study of dechristianization cannot be dissociated from the study of society as a whole, proving once again that there is no such thing as a religious history apart from a history of man.

Pontien Polman, O. F. M./*Utrecht, Netherlands*

Historical Background of Old Catholicism

I

THE CHURCH OF UTRECHT

Old Catholicism as we know it today is the communion of those who reject, since 1870, the dogma of papal infallibility, particularly in Germany, and the "Roman-Catholic Church of the Old Episcopal Clergy" (roughly: Dutch Jansenists) whose principal see had already been established in Utrecht a century and a half ago.[1] These predominantly German Catholics, disappointed by the attitude of their own bishops and hopeful of organizing their movement on a Catholic basis, which was not

---

[1] The Vicar Apostolic of Holland, Petrus Codde, refused to sign the "Formulier" (statement), was suspended in 1702 and deposed in 1704. A part of the clergy could not accept this papal intervention in the affairs of their Church, and this led to the election of a bishop in 1723, who was ordained two years later by a suspended French prelate. This was the beginning of the episcopal succession which continues up to the present. Leaving Dutch literature aside, I refer, for broader orientation, to two studies which have dealt with the schism of Utrecht in the framework of the history of ideas: on the non-Catholic side there is C. B. Moss, *The Old-Catholic Movement. Its Origins and History* (London, 1948), and on the Catholic side, G. Leclercq, *Zeger Bernard van Espen et l'autorité ecclésiastique* (Zürich, 1964). Moss situates the schism in the general development of ideas which led to the Old Catholicism of 1870. Leclercq is more specialized; his canonical study, on a sound historical basis, contains an excellent survey (pp. 86-105) of the history of this schism (1702-1725) and the important part played by the Louvain professor Van Espen as adviser in this development.

possible without the charisma of ordination, turned to the bishops of the Church of Utrecht who ordained their candidate.

This had no less important consequences for the Church of Utrecht itself, for it meant the end of its isolation. In 1889 it linked up with some Old Catholic communions and concluded the "Union of Utrecht" (based on the Declaration of Utrecht) which did not affect the autonomy of the individual national Churches. Since then it has also adopted the name "Old Catholic". Under the influence of its relations with these far more radically inclined Churches, the Church of Utrecht gradually changed on various points the traditional attitude which had kept alive its hope of reunion with Rome. Lastly, in ecumenical matters this Church has begun to play its part in the World Council of Churches where it leans more readily toward episcopal communions. As a result it has accepted *intercommunio in sacris* with the Anglicans.

II

THE SCHISM OF UTRECHT

The question of papal infallibility had already been a factor when the schism of the Church of Utrecht took place in 1723, insofar as it came to the fore in the dealings with Jansenism. For the real cause lay in the difference of opinion on the pope's primacy: the conflict between the national and the universal Church, in other words, between those that affirmed and those that denied the pope's supreme jurisdiction over every diocese and over all dioceses collectively. These are the problems which are usually designated by the vague and elastic name of Gallicanism. In this case the question was whether the pope had the right to depose a vicar apostolic or a bishop. The reason why the pope decided to do so lies on another level.

The incubation period of the schism began with the suspension of Peter Codde in 1702, which was followed by his deposition in 1704. The soul of the opposition, both in theory and in practice, was the erudite parish priest of Delft, Joan Christiaan van Erkel, who dealt with the principles of the question in 1702 and 1703,[2] and was supported by Egidius de Witte, a no less erudite Fleming who had fled to Holland. Criticizing the interpretation which saw in the "thou art Peter" text an argument in favor of the primacy, they emphasized the collegiate bond of the apostles whose successors are the bishops. It is they who have supreme authority within the boundaries of a diocese, and the early Christian Church is the model for their relationship with each other, with the metropolitan and with the bishop of Rome. In connection with this argument these authors use the concept of the sovereignty of the people, they reject the monarchical structure of the Church, and allow the pope only a primacy of honor. The pope's conduct toward Peter Codde was therefore unlawful.

De Witte's Theory

De Witte wrote as follows: "The Church is not a monarchy, of which the pope is the king and the bishops the subjects or vassals; the Church is a spiritual Commonwealth, governed by the nobility under one Chief. . . . In order to understand the full meaning of this, one should realize that the keys of the Church, in other words, the government of the Church, were given by Christ to the whole Church, that is, to the apostolic college, in which the whole Church is symbolized as in her princely nobility. . . . The full episcopal power to govern the Church was given by Christ to the apostles collectively and to their heirs equally and indivisibly. And therefore this power does not originally belong to the pope in Rome (as some think

[2] J. C. van Erkel, *Berigt aan de Rooms-Catholyken om aan haer te vertonen hoe ze haer moeten gedragen omtrent pauselijke ofte Roomse beveelen* door N.N.P. (Anno 1702). *Assertio juris Ecclesiae Metropolitanae Ultrajectinae Romano-Catholicae* per J. C. E(rkelicum) (Delft, 1703).

wrongly) but to the whole council of the Church's guardians or
the whole spiritual authority as instituted by Christ."[3]

Up to his death in 1732 Van Erkel, the spiritual father of the
schism, occupied himself indefatigably with working out these
ideas on national lines and with gathering evidence from the
history of civil and canon law. In this he was assisted by Quesnel[4]
among others. It was a matter of providing a basis for the maintenance of the medieval liberties of the Dutch Church, such as
the *ius de non evocando* and the right of *placet,* and of proving
to contemporaries that the hierarchy of 1559 had not been ousted
by the establishment of Calvinism; that the Dutch Church was
not a mission Church and still in possession of its episcopal sees
and its chapters; that the vicars apostolic were in fact the Or-
dinaries of Utrecht; that the chapters had a say in the appoint-
ments of bishops and had full jurisdiction *sede vacante.* The
pope had to respect these rights and could not arbitrarily impose
an ecclesiastical administrator on the Dutch.

Appeal to Civic Authorities

These ideas did not remain pure theory. As soon as it became
known that Codde had been suspended and a substitute had been
appointed, Van Erkel appealed to the civic authorities, the Cal-
vinist States of Holland. By decree of August 17, 1702, these
authorities forbade the substitute to exercise his function and
declared that in the future the ecclesiastical administrator would
have to be chosen from among the native clergy, and by them,
if he wanted to be sure of their silent approval.[5] It would therefore no longer be a matter of suggesting candidates to the pope,
as had been the case till then, but to the States; in other words,

---

[3] Desiderius Paleophilus (E. de Witte), *Afbeelding van de pauselijke
waerdigheyd, alwaer hetgene den Paus van regtswegen toekomt, of niet
toe en komt, volgens de H. Schriftuur en Kerkelyke Overlevering met
bondige getuygenissen bewesen word* (Anno 1704, 1709, 1712). This
appeared also in Latin: *Imago pontificiae dignitatis.*

[4] J. Tans, *Pasquier Quesnel et les Pays-Bas* (Groningen, 1960), p. 363.

[5] See my article, "Cleresie en Staatsgezag. Het plakkaat van 17 augus-
tus 1702," in *Mededelingen van het Nederlands Historisch Instituut te
Rome* IX (1957), pp. 163-89.

it was no longer the civic authority but the ecclesiastical one that would be faced with a *fait accompli*. All that is expected of the pope is that he approve the candidate of the clerical body which has obtained the *placet* from the States; a candidate directly nominated by the pope would no longer stand a chance. This henceforth excluded Rome's influence from the affairs of the Dutch Church. One can understand that the States were prepared to support such a nationally based Catholicism. Hence every measure the pope wanted to take with regard to the Dutch Church was immediately followed by a countermeasure taken by the States on the advice of Van Erkel.

Such a situation had been unknown in Holland up till then. To whom Van Erkel and De Witte owed their opinions is difficult to say. It is not likely that they took them from Zeger Bernard van Espen, a professor of Louvain University who only then began to develop these notions for the use of the clerical movement. They were certainly not shared by Peter Codde and, to my knowledge, do not appear in contemporary literature outside the writings of these two protagonists. The "Cleresie" or Jansenist clerical movement was still a movement without program; systematic formation on the basis of principles probably started with the foundation of a seminary at Amersfoort. During the incubation period those dissatisfied with the pope's conduct toward Codde automatically ranged themselves behind the spokesmen without bothering too much about the theory and without being aware of the consequences. This happened the more easily as nobody thought of a separation. Thus they slipped naturally into the schismatic situation when circumstances were favorable to this development, that is, when a bishop was found who was prepared to transmit the power of ordination to the candidate of the "Cleresie", as happened in 1723. Of the 396 secular clergy then active in Holland 75 were known to support the party,[6] a figure based on their conduct; how many of these were also doctrinally convinced it is impossible to ascertain.

[6] Thus the Vicar Apostolic, Joan van Bijlevelt, in his report of 1724; see my publication, *Romeinse bronnen* IV (The Hague, 1955), n.810.

III

BLAME FOR THE SCHISM

Utrecht's View

According to the group of Utrecht the blame for the schism lay with Rome. When a chapter elects a bishop it exercises a right and Rome has but to confirm the choice. Rome, on the other hand, maintained that there was no chapter in Utrecht and that Utrecht made claims which conflict with ancient national law and the *Concordata Germaniae*. Yet, Utrecht clung to the venerable tradition of asking for Rome's approval and of maintaining close relations with the bishops and chapters of neighboring Churches. Soon Van Erkel started to send them copies of his writings and to warn them against the presumptions of Rome: "Your own interests are at stake when your neighbor's house is burning" (*Iam tua res agitur, paries dum proximus ardet*). In this way he puts the Church of Utrecht on the same level as those of Antwerp, Malines, Roermond, Cologne and Münster. The prelates of these Sees had been regularly informed of the elections to the See of Utrecht, just as the bishop of Rome. Whether, or how, they react is for the rest of no importance. This did not prevent Utrecht from hoping to receive as many letters as possible attesting ecclesiastical communion and adhesion to their movement. These were then published in a few *Recueils de témoignage*. Out of all this grew the theory that, in spite of everything, there was indirect contact with Rome, namely through the relations with those that were subject to Rome.

Rome's View

According to Rome, the blame for the schism lay with Utrecht. The primacy of the pope was already so clearly defined by the Council of Florence in 1439 that the Council of 1870 only had to take over the formula. No dogma has met with such rigid and prolonged opposition, for reasons of practice or principle, because no dogma is so pregnant with consequences and repercussions in the sphere of temporal interests. One has but to remember the nomination of bishops. Generally speaking, there had been two doctrinal tendencies in Europe for centuries: in the North the Council of Florence was not generally accepted as ecumenical, and the influence of the Councils of Constance and Basle persisted; in the South the teaching about the primacy was fully developed. In Holland both the "Gallican" and Ultramontane tendencies were alive at the beginning of the 18th century, as we have already seen.

The attitude of the pope was determined by circumstances. In the case of a prince who considered religion a divinely entrusted task, or an interest of the State, the best tactics were to temporize. One form of absolutism could not tolerate another by its side. Thus in practice the pope directly nominated only ecclesiastical administrators in mission lands between about 1648 and 1795, while everywhere else this was done by the ruler, often by a concordat concluded at the expense of the local chapters. But all danger of a rupture of Church unity disappeared when Louis XIV began to repudiate the *Déclaration* of 1682, and Joseph II revoked his reform measures, forced by the revolution of Brabant. However, Church authorities, inclined to greater independence from Rome, had still to rely on secular power if they wanted to achieve anything. When this support failed, was refused or revoked, they were exposed to condemnation, as Febronius, the archbishops of the Rhineland and the Fathers of the Synod of Pistoia found out. In the same way, it is likely that many who were sympathetic to the "Cleresie" during the 18th century had good reasons not to follow its example. In fact, nowhere did Gallicanism lead to a schism except in the case of Utrecht.

State Support

The remarkable privilege of maintaining, by relying on State support, an independence beyond the reach of papal displeasure, is shared by the Church of Utrecht and the Society of Jesus— interesting bedfellows. In the case of the Church of Utrecht the burden of this difficult situation was borne principally by the protégés. The pope would never be prepared to leave the nomination of a Vicar for Holland in the hands of a Protestant power with which he had no relations whatever. Only too soon he would be asked to approve a candidate he thought he would have to excommunicate. Apart from other considerations the pope may have had, the spirit of the age happened to be the spirit of absolutism: people thought in terms of authority and subjection. At the start of the conflict much was written on whether one should obey the pope or the State. Without hesitation Van Erkel and De Witte opted for the State.

IV

PAPAL PREROGATIVES AND EPISCOPAL COLLEGIALITY

When Van Erkel takes the Church of the first five centuries as the norm and the Church of the first ten as the norm accepted by the Union of Utrecht, there is no real difference because in both cases he means the undivided Christian Church. The pattern was taken from contemporary inter-confessional polemics and was current in the days of Van Erkel when Bossuet, in his *Variations,* branded as error any change in religious matters; when Nicole did the same thing from another point of view in his *Perpétuité de la foy,* and when they were imitated by the third "Father of the Church" of Utrecht, Hugo van Heussen.[7] Taking a certain fixity as its norm, the "Cleresie" of the early 18th century rejected any development in doctrine or discipline as a symptom of degeneracy, and aimed at curing the situation by a return to the past.

The fact that during the Middle Ages the teaching about the bishop's function was left far behind the teaching about the papacy may be explained by the prolonged decline in episcopal status. When at long last the helmet and sword were abandoned

[7] F. van Staden (H. van Heussen), *Handt- en huysboek der Katholyken, waarin de voornaamste geloofsstukken verdedigd worden* (Leiden, 1703), pp. 67-75 and 584-850.

for the miter and crosier it was too late to catch up with the arrears. Throughout the age of absolutism—which left its marks —while the defenders of the primacy steered toward infallibility, those that risked a good word in favor of the apostolic college and the bishop's place in the universal and local Church were suspected of hobnobbing with heresy. In the eyes of the Ultra-montanists, Bossuet, for instance, was far from innocent, not to mention such convinced episcopalists as Van Espen and Fe-bronius. But when the teaching on papal prerogatives had reached a climax in 1870, the direction in which theological thought about episcopal collegiality could develop became clear.

PART IV

CHRONICLE OF THE
LIVING CHURCH

IN COLLABORATION WITH
KATHOLIEK ARCHIEF
Amersfoort, Netherlands

A "Dialogue" between Christian and Marxist Scholars

The evening of April 29, 1965, saw the opening in Salzburg of a three-day congress, organized by the Paulus Society and described as the "first great colloquy" between Christians and Marxists by R. Garaudy, Director of the Center of Marxist Study and Research in Paris. The theme of this congress, "Christianity and Marxism Today", attracted so much public interest that the Society was forced to lift its usual restrictions and allow many to take part in the event as guests or reporters.

The intention of the Paulus Society was to bring Christians and Marxists together on an international level, not as a political event but for scholarly discussion. This was in accordance with the nature of the Society which had always viewed its role during ten years of its existence as a free forum for discussion and exchange of ideas. Christian and Marxist scholars were invited to forget for once the harsh realities of political action and to discuss together on the platform the question of whether Christianity and Marxism are really as irreconcilable—at least in theory —as they appear to be today. The three aspects to be dealt with during the three days of discussion were: Man and Religion, the Future of Mankind, and Ideological Coexistence.

Many Church and party leaders of East and West objected that the time was not ripe for such an undertaking, or condemned the project as utopian or bound to fail. Such objections, however, inspired by harsh political reality, did not reach the discussion stage. They were outweighed by the fact that the Paulus Society is dedicated to science, humanity and man's self-respect, which force man to account for himself as a rational being if he does not want to yield to ultimate self-rejection; and by the fact that the large number of scientists in the Society, along with the help of ethical contributions, strongly felt the need of more exchange of information in order to avoid a faulty analysis of the present and a wrong orientation of the future.

As the congress proceeded, it became evident that the Paulus Society could make only a bare beginning. Rather than dialogue, long stretches of the meeting seemed to be a series of previously prepared monologues, and lacked the flexibility and spontaneity which lend color and substance to a conversation. Those who listened to the many papers of varying quality produced by both the Marxist and Christian representatives, will agree that there was little or no genuine dialogue on the platform in Salzburg. It became clear what vast distances separated the speakers even in their terminology. It became equally clear that future possibilities of contact do not lie in rhetorical monologues, but—if at all—in the regular meeting of qualified people in small working groups. The pre-conciliar working groups on Christian unity might well serve as a model. The readiness to respond to such constructive discussions in comparative seclusion might be the test of the sincerity of those who so loudly proclaim, in impressive public congresses, their willingness to cooperate.

A "Societas Liturgica" in Process of Formation

Agroup of European and American theologians and churchmen met for study and discussion of liturgical matters (March 22-26, 1965) at the home of the Community of Grandchamp, near Neuchâtel, Switzerland. The European initiators were the Rev. Wiebe Vos (Rotterdam), Editor of *Studia Liturgica* since its inception in 1962, and Professor J. J. von Allmen, Professor of Practical Theology at the University of Neuchâtel. Chief spokesman for the North American representatives was Canon Don H. Copeland, Director of the newly founded World Center for Liturgical Studies at Boca Raton, Florida. Attendance was by invitation, and participants included Anglicans, Baptists, Lutherans, Methodists, Orthodox, Reformed, and Roman Catholics.

The conference had both a study theme and a practical task: to further the discussion on Christian Initiation, and to make provision for continued collaboration in matters concerning liturgical research and life.

On Christian Initiation the following papers were presented and discussed:

(1) "The Relation between Baptism, Confirmation and the Eucharist in the pre-Nicene Church, from an Historical Viewpoint," (Geoffry Wainwright, Methodist Church, England).

173

(2) "The Rite of Initiation in the Syrian Orthodox Church in India, from a Theological Viewpoint," (Dr. Paul Verghese, Syrian Orthodox Church).

(3) "The Theology of Confirmation in Relation to Baptism and the Eucharist: Recent Trends in the Swiss Reformed Churches," (Pastor Richard Paquier, Swiss Protestant Church Federation).

(4) "The Theology of Confirmation in Relation to Baptism and the Eucharist: Recent Trends in Roman Catholicism," (Th. Vismans, O.P., Roman Catholic Church, the Netherlands).

(5) "Confirmation: Problems and Experiments in the German Evangelical Church," (Pastor Walter Lotz, Evangelical Church in Germany).

(6) "Confirmation: Problems and Experiments in the Church of England," (Dr. Gilbert Cope, the Church of England).

Among other topics for common study (a), and projects for common labor (b), the following were suggested:

(a) The presence of Christ in the liturgy of the Word; the eucharistic sacrifice; the place of Mary in worship; the commemoration of the saints and the departed; the theology of the priesthood; the architectural setting of worship; the Church's ministry to the sick; liturgy and mission; liturgy and society; the meaning and practice of penance; the relation between liturgy and "Lehre"; a total theology focused in liturgy; Church music; glossolalia, improvisation, and silence in worship; the indigenization of worship; the place and function of liturgical education in seminaries, including the provision of adequate textbooks.

(b) The ecumenical study of the lectionary and calendar leading to possible agreement in usage; collaboration on the daily office and on the eucharistic prayer; a Protestant review of the question of the regularity of the eucharistic celebration.

During the time of its meeting the conference worshiped in varied fashion: members joined with the Sisters of Grandchamp in their daily office; compline was said nightly; the eucharist was celebrated each morning, the first day by means of the *Evangelische Messe* according to the Michaelsbruderschaft, the second day the Roman Catholic mass as shaped by Vatican II, the third day according to the Birmingham experimental rite. A report on the conference, together with some of the papers, will be published in *Studia Liturgia* 3 (1965).

Regarding the continuation of liturgical work, the meeting resolved to form a *Societas Liturgica* for "the promoting of the ecumenical dialogue on worship, based on solid research and with the perspective of renewal and unity". The detailed elaboration of a constitution was left to a commission of fifteen members, which met in Strasbourg on May 31 and June 1. Among other things there has been stipulated that "the aim of the *Societas* shall be the furtherance of liturgical study and practice through appropriate means such as exchange of information, congresses, etc." (Art. 3). The first ecumenical world congress on liturgical studies, organized by the *Societas Liturgica,* will be held in Oxford, September 12 to 16, 1966. Subscriptions and further information may be obtained from Pastor Wiebe Vos, Mathenesserlaan 301 c, Rotterdam, the Netherlands.

BIOGRAPHICAL NOTES

BRIAN TIERNEY: Born May 1, 1922 in Scunthorpe, England. He studied at Cambridge University, and earned his doctorate in 1951. He received an honorary Doctor of Theology degree at the University of Uppsala in 1964. He taught at the Catholic University of America until 1959, and since then has been Professor of Medieval History at Cornell University. He is at present President of the American Catholic Historical Association. His published works include *Foundations of the Conciliar Theory* (1955), *Medieval Poor Law* (1959) and *The Crisis of Church and State, 1050-1300* (1964).

HILAIRE MAROT, O.S.B.: Born October 14, 1920. He became a Benedictine, and pursued his studies at the University of Paris and at the Collegio San Anselmo in Rome, earning degrees in theology and history. He is a regular contributor to various reviews, notably *Irenikon*, and has contributed to several symposia.

AUGUST FRANZEN: Born February 12, 1912 in Wuppertal, Germany, he was ordained in 1937 for the diocese of Cologne. He studied at the University of Bonn, at the Gregorian University in Rome, and at the Scuola Palaeographica (Vatican), earning his doctorate in theology in 1939, and a licentiate in canon law in 1948. After working in a parish for eight years, he taught theology at the seminary in Bonn from 1949 to 1956, was a Professor of Theology at the University of Bonn until 1960 when he came to his present post as Professor of Church History at the University of Freiburg. His published works include frequent contributions to historical reviews.

GIUSEPPE ALBERIGO: Born January 21, 1926 in Varese, Italy. He studied at the Catholic University of Milan, earning his doctorate in jurisprudence in 1948. He is Associate Professor of Church History and Professor of Philosophy at the University of Florence, and also Secretary to the Centro di Documentazione-Instituto per le Scienze Religiose in Bologna. His published works deal with Church government and history, and he is a regular contributor to ecclesiastical and historical reviews.

ROGER AUBERT: Born in 1914 in Ixelles-Brussels, he is today a doctor of philosophy and theology. After teaching in the seminary at Malines, Belgium, from 1944 to 1952, he came to his present post at the University of Louvain, where he teaches church history. In 1945 he published his doctoral thesis, "Le problème de l'acte de foi". His numerous activities and many published works concentrate upon the problems of contemporary church history. Examples are: *Le Saint Siège et l'union des Eglises: Le Pontificat de Pie IX* (Vol. XXI in Fliche-Martin); *La théologie catholique au milieu du XXe siècle* (1953); *Problèmes de l'unité chrétienne* (1955); *Le concile du Vatican* (Vol. XII in *l'Histoire des conciles oecuméniques* edited by G. Dumeige, 1964).

JACQUES FERNAND FONTAINE: Born April 25, 1922 in Les Lilas, France, he studied at the Sorbonne and at the Ecole des Hautes Etudes Hispaniques. He earned a degree in literature in 1943, and his doctorate in 1957. He was Professor of Literature at Caen before taking his present post as Professor of Latin Languages and Literature at the Sorbonne in 1958. He has several published works to his credit, and is a frequent contributor to a number of reviews.

ANTON GERARD WEILER: Born November 6, 1927. He studied at the Catholic University of Nijmegen, Netherlands, at the Ecole des Chartes and the Ecole des Hautes Etudes in Paris. He earned a degree in philosophy in 1952, and his doctorate in history in 1962. Since 1959 he has been a member of the Catholic Faculty at Tilburg, and in 1964 became Professor of History, Paleography and Diplomacy at the University of Nijmegen. His published works include lectures on Medieval and Renaissance History, and contributions to *The New Catholic Encyclopedia* and *Lexikon für Theologie und Kirche*.

HERMANN TÜCHLE: Born November 7, 1905 in Esslinger, Germany, he was ordained in 1930 for the diocese of Rottenburg. He studied at the University of Tübingen where he earned his doctorate in theology in 1937, and became a lecturer in theology in 1939. He later taught at the University of Paderborn, and since 1952 he has been Professor of Church History at the University of Munich. His published works include *Kirchengeschichte* (together with Bihlmeyer); he was the editor of *Die eine Kirche* (1939), and the third volume of his *Geschichte der Kirche* appeared earlier this year. He is a well-known contributor to a number of theological reviews.

RENÉ RÉMOND: Born September 30, 1918 in Lons-le-Saunier, France, he studied at the Ecole Normal Superieur, took a degree in history and earned his doctorate in 1959. He is a Professor in the Faculty of Literature and Humanities in Paris, and Director of Studies and Research at the Fondation Nationale des Sciences Politiques. He is the author of several published works, and a regular contributor to reviews in the fields of history and political science.

PONTIEN POLMAN, O.F.M.: Born August 20, 1897 in Amsterdam, Netherlands, he became a Franciscan and was ordained in 1922. He studied at
the University of Louvain, and earned his doctorate in theology in 1927.
He was Professor of Church History at Alverna from 1927 to 1954. His
published works include *L'Element historique dans la controverse religieuse du XVIe siècle* (Gembloux, 1932). He contributes regularly to the
Revue d'Histoire Ecclesiastique.

International Publishers of CONCILIUM

ENGLISH EDITION
Paulist Press
Glen Rock, N. J., U.S.A.

Burns & Oates Ltd.
25 Ashley Place
London, S.W.1

DUTCH EDITION
Uitgeverij Paul Brand, N. V.
Hilversum, Netherlands

FRENCH EDITION
Maison Mame
Tours/Paris, France

GERMAN EDITION
Verlagsanstalt Benziger & Co., A.G.
Einsiedeln, Switzerland

Matthias Grunewald-Verlag
Mainz, W. Germany

SPANISH EDITION
Ediciones Guadarrama
Madrid, Spain

PORTUGUESE EDITION
Livraria Morais Editora, Ltda.
Lisbon, Portugal

ITALIAN EDITION
Editrice Queriniana
Brescia, Italy